John Wilbur Chapman, William Phillips Hall

Christian Hymns, No. 1

For Use in Church Services, Sunday-schools, Young People's Societies, etc.

John Wilbur Chapman, William Phillips Hall

Christian Hymns, No. 1
For Use in Church Services, Sunday-schools, Young People's Societies, etc.

ISBN/EAN: 9783337083052

Printed in Europe, USA, Canada, Australia, Japan

Cover: Foto ©Thomas Meinert / pixelio.de

More available books at **www.hansebooks.com**

FOR USE IN

Church Services, Sunday-Schools,
Young People's Societies, Etc. . .

COMPILED BY

WILLIAM PHILLIPS HALL

AND

REV. J. WILBUR CHAPMAN, D. D.

EDITOR OF MUSIC:

W. S. WEEDEN.

HALL-MACK CO.,

PUBLISHERS,

1020 Arch Street, Philadelphia, Pa.

PREFACE.

THIS Hymn Book has been prepared after the most careful and prayerful thought. For a number of years as Evangelists and Christian workers we have been brought in contact with the different Churches and feel that we know their need, and it is to help meet this in common with other Hymn Books that this collection of CHRISTIAN HYMNS is sent forth. We have designed it for use in the Church, and with this fact in mind many of the old Standard hymns, together with very many new ones, have been chosen. We have had in our minds the special work of the Sunday-school, and believe we have some of the best Sunday-school hymns published, in our collection. We have not forgotten the Young People's Societies of the Churches, and have at considerable expense secured some of the most inspiring hymns we know. In addition to all this we feel perfectly confident that Evangelists and Pastors engaged in special meetings will find just such hymns as would be an inspiration in their work, and in addition to all this such Responsive Readings have been chosen as make the book useful in any service of any character, in all the work of the Church. With a prayer that the Hymn Book may be a blessing, we send it forth on its mission of song.

NEW YORK CITY, N. Y., October, 1899.

CHRISTIAN HYMNS, No. 1.

JESUS ALL THE WAY.

FLORA KIRKLAND.   Isaiah 41: 10.   W. S. WEEDEN.

Respectfully dedicated to my friend, Wm. Phillips Hall, Greenwich, Conn.

1. I am walking thro' this earth-life, Oft- en wea - ry, oft - en sad;
2. I am trav'ling to a cit - y Where the light is nev - er dim,
3. I am looking for re - demption Thro' the mer- its of my King;

But my Saviour walketh with me, And his presence makes me glad.
And my Saviour leads so gent - ly, It is sweet to walk with him.
Bless- ed beams of free sal - va - tion Shine a- bout me as I sing.

CHORUS.

Je - sus knoweth ev - 'ry sor - row, Je - sus knoweth ev - 'ry fear;

And he whispers thro' life's shadows, "Do not tremble, I am near!"

No. 4.   THE INNER CIRCLE.

Dedicated to Rev. J. Wilbur Chapman, D. D., and first sung in the Union Meetings at Mount Vernon in November 1898.

FLORA KIRKLAND.   W. S. WEEDEN.

1. Have you heard the voice of Je - sus Whisper, "I have chosen you?"
2. As the first dis - ci- ples followed, As they went where'er he sent;
3. Or, if he shall choose to send us On some er - rand in his name,
4. Master, at thy foot-stool kneeling, We, thy children, humbly wait;

Does he tell you in commun - ion What he wish - es you to do?
So to - day we, too, may fol - low, On his lead - ing still in - tent.
We can serve him as dis - ci - ples, For our place is just the same.
Lead us, send us, bless us, use us, Till we en - ter heaven's gate.

CHORUS.

Are you in the in - ner cir - cle? Have you heard the Master's call?
Are you in the in - ner cir - cle? Have you heard the Master's call?

Have you giv'n your life to Je - sus? Is he now your All in all?
Have you giv'n your

No. 5. "SAVED TO SAVE OTHERS."

Flora Kirkland. Chas. H. Gabriel.

1. "Saved to save others," rejoicing, I sing; Lord be my Teacher to-day!
2. Life's little moment is hast'ning away, Come to the Master, O come!
3. Sin is al-luring; but how will it end? Powers of e-vil are strong?
4. Master, thy mercy has reached even me, Help me show others the way;

Help me lead someone to heaven's pure spring, Help me show someone the way.
Come to him now, while 'tis yet called "to-day," Come, heavy-laden one, come!
Come to the sinners' unchangeable Friend, He giveth vict'ry and song.
Up to the fountain of mercy so free Help me lead someone to-day.

Chorus.

"Saved to save others" to-day!...... Saved to show others the way!......
to save others!   to show others!
to-day!   the way!

Lord, keep me faithful, and fill me with pow'r, Fill me, and use me, I pray.

No. 6.   COUNT YOUR BLESSINGS.

Rev. JOHNSON OATMAN, Jr.

E. O. EXCELL.

1. When up - on life's billows you are tempest toss'd, When you are discouraged,
2. Are you ev - er burdened with a load of care? Does the cross seem heavy
3. When you look at others with their lands and gold, Think that Christ has promised
4. So a - mid the conflict, whether great or small, Do not be discouraged,

thinking all is lost, Count your ma-ny blessings, name them one by one,
you are called to bear? Count your ma-ny blessings, ev - 'ry doubt will fly,
you his wealth un-told, Count your ma-ny blessings, mon-ey can - not buy
God is o - ver all; Count your ma-ny blessings, an-gels will at- tend,

CHORUS.

And it will surprise you, what the Lord hath done. Count your blessings, Name them
And you will be singing as the days go by.
Your reward in heaven, nor your home on high.
Help and comfort give you to your journey's end.

Count your many blessings,

one by one, Count your blessings, See what God hath done: Count your
Name them one by one, Count your many blessings, See what God hath done; Count your many

blessings, Name them one by one, Count your many blessings, See what God hath done.

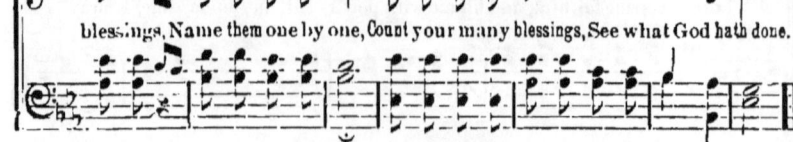

No. 7.   THE SCARLET LINE.

FLORA KIRKLAND.   W. S. WEEDEN.

1. The paschal lambs in   silence pointed To Christ, the cru - ci - fied,
2. The prophet's thirty   sil - ver piec - es Point on to   that dark   night
3. The types are shining out their meaning, They point us to   the   Lamb;

The first one, long be - fore his birth-night, The last, be - fore he   died.
When, as a slave, for thir - ty piec - es Was sold the Lord of   light.
The bush that burned and yet consumed not Foretold the great "I   Am."

The blood was sprinkled o'er the door-ways Above, on eith - er   side,
The thrilling words that David uttered 'Ere Bethl'hem's Babe was born
We fol- low out, in wondrous de - tail, His sorrow, shame and loss;

Fine.

The shadow of   the cross on Cal- v'ry, Whence flowed the healing tide.
Tell e - ven of the parted garments On Calv'ry's day of   scorn.
We find on all the sa - cred pag - es The shadow of the cross.

D.S.—Connecting proph-e - cy with Je - sus; It proves the Book di - vine.

CHORUS.   D.S.

A scarlet line thro' Scripture runneth, A wondrous scar - let line,

No. 8.   PERFECT TRUST IN THEE.

FANNIE J. CROSBY.   ALVIN S. CLARK.

1. I ask O Lord,.............. that thou will lead,.............. My err - ing
2. I do not ask.............. a cloud- less sky,.............. Nor yet a
3. I would not seek.............. in i - dle mirth,.......... To still one
4. O clothe me in.................. thy righteousness,.............. Hold thou my

1. I ask O Lord,   that thou wilt lead,

steps   a - right,........... I ask for grace.............. that I may
path   of rest,.............. But strength to climb....... the rugged
throb   of care,............. For what are all.............. the joys of
hand   in thine,........... And teach my heart.......... in faith to

my err - ing steps, my err-ing steps a-right,   I ask for grace,

walk............ By faith,................ and not by sight............
steep,........... Thy wea - ry feet have pressed.......
earth,.......... With-out.............. thy presence there?..........
say,............ Thy will,.............. O Lord, not mine...........

that I may walk, By faith, and not by sight,   By faith, and not by sight.

CHORUS.

O let the language of my heart, In each pe-tition be...... "Take what thou

wilt,........... but grant me this,........ A per-fect trust in thee."

"Take what thou wilt,   but grant me this,

Copyright, 1899, by Wm. J. Kirkpatrick.

No. 9.   LEANING ON THE EVERLASTING ARMS.

Rev. E. A. HOFFMAN.   A. J. SHOWALTER.

1. What a fel-lowship, what a joy di-vine, Lean-ing on the ev-er-
2. Oh, how sweet to walk in this pil-grim way, Lean-ing on the ev-er-
3. What have I to dread, what have I to fear, Lean-ing on the ev-er-

last-ing arms; What a bless-ed-ness, what a peace is mine,
last-ing arms; Oh, how bright the path grows from day to day,
last-ing arms? I have bless-ed peace with my Lord so near,

REFRAIN.

Lean-ing on the ev-er-last-ing arms.)
Lean-ing on the ev-er-last-ing arms. } Lean - - ing,
Lean-ing on the ev-er-last-ing arms.)   Lean-ing on Je-sus,

lean - - - ing,   Safe and se-cure from all a-larms;
Lean - ing on Je - sus,

Lean - ing,   lean - ing,   Leaning on the ev-er-last-ing arms.
Lean-ing on Je-sus,   lean-ing on Je-sus,

No. 10.   IT DOTH NOT YET APPEAR.

Rev. Wm. Stone.   C. Austin Miles.

1. All doubt has left my troubled soul, Sweet peace, now reigns with-in;
2. Is this a fore-taste of that bliss; 'Tis heav'n be-gun be-low,
3. I'll hast-en on to meet him then; I long to see his face:

I have no fear, that conflict's o'er, My heart is cleansed from sin.
O! rapturous joy, that thrills my heart, A Sav-iour thus to know.
To hear him say, "well done my child, A tri-umph of my grace."

CHORUS.

Bless-ed peace, doth fill me now, My soul is thrilled with cheer;

But what I shall be when he comes It doth not yet ap-pear.

4 What will it be to meet him there,
    Whose blood hath set me free,
To look upon those wounded hands,
    He bore on Calvary.

5 O! Saviour dear, I come, I come,
    To spend eternity;
With thee, who didst my ransom pay,
    In bitterest agony.

No. 11.   MY SAVIOUR FIRST OF ALL.

FANNY J. CROSBY.   JNO. R. SWENEY.

1. When my life-work is end-ed, and I cross the swell-ing tide, When the
2. Oh, the soul-thrilling rapture when I view his bless-ed face, And the
3. Oh, the dear ones in glo-ry, how they beck-on me to come, And our
4. Thro' the gates to the cit-y in a robe of spot-less white, He will

bright and glorious morning I shall see; I shall know my Re-deem-er when I
lus-tre of his kindly beaming eye; How my full heart will praise him for the
parting at the riv-er I re-call; To the sweet vales of E-den they will
lead me where no tears will ever fall; In the glad song of a-ges I shall

reach the oth-er side, And his smile will be the first to welcome me.
mer-cy, love, and grace, That prepares for me a mansion in the sky.
sing my wel-come home; But I long to meet my Saviour first of all.
min-gle with de-light; But I long to meet my Saviour first of all.

CHORUS.

I shall know him, I shall know him, And redeem'd by his side I shall stand,
I shall know him,

I shall know him, I shall know him By the print of the nails in his hand.
I shall know him,

COUNT THY MERCIES.

E. A. H.

REV. ELISHA A. HOFFMAN.

1. Ev'ry day new mercies greet thee; Ev'ry day new joys are thine:
2. O how man-i-fold God's blessings! More than thou canst number o'er;
3. Not a good his hand with-hold-eth; Not a joy his love de-nies;
4. Shall we not be grateful to him For his mercies man-i-fold,

Gifts of heaven's lov-ing-kind-ness; Tokens of the love di-vine.
Yet in kindness he be-stow-eth Dai-ly mercies more and more.
Each new blessing he un-fold-eth Fills our hearts with new surprise.
And in each new gift he sends us All his wondrous grace be-hold?

CHORUS.

Count thy mercies, count them o-ver, Count the blessings God has giv'n;

And for all his lov-ing-kind-ness Grateful be to God in heav'n.

No. 13. SALVATION.

E. RICKMAN.

W. S. WEEDEN.

1. Hark! the gracious proc-la-mation Sounding o-ver earth and sea;
2. Hear his lov-ing in-vi-ta-tion, "Heavy lad-en, come to me;"
3. Linger not! for night is fall-ing; "Tarry not in all the plain:"
4. Higher than the heav'ns above thee Is the mer-cy of the Lord.
5. Hear the gos-pel in-vi-ta-tion Sounding o-ver earth and sea:

'Tis the Saviour's in-vi-ta-tion: Burdened one, 'tis offered thee;
Still he of-fers free sal-va-tion, For he bled and died for thee:
Linger not! for Christ is call-ing; Shall he plead with thee in vain?
Lonely heart, there's One to love thee—One by an-gel-host a-dored.
Par-don, rec-on-cil-i-a-tion, Full sal-va-tion—full and free.

Life is drear-y, Thou art wea-ry; Hear his message, "Come to me;"
Sin con-fess-ing, Claim the blessing, Take his gift and happy be!
Oft re-ject-ed, Long neglect-ed, Yet he calls thee once a-gain;
He will take thee, Ne'er forsake thee Till the lost one is restored;
Je-sus bought it, Have you sought it? Take this gift and hap-py be!

Life is drear-y, Thou art wea-ry; Hear his message, "Come to me."
Sin con-fess-ing, Claim the blessing, Take his gift and happy be!
Oft re-ject-ed, Long neglect-ed, Yet he calls thee once a-gain.
He will take thee, Ne'er forsake thee Till the lost one is restored.
Je-sus bought it, Have you sought it? Take this gift and hap-py be!

No. 14. **HIGHER GROUND.**

Rev. Johnson Oatman, Jr.   Chas. H. Gabriel.

1. I'm pressing on   the upward way, New heights I'm gaining ev'ry day;
2. My heart has no   de-sire to   stay Where doubts arise and fears dismay;
3. I   want to live   above the world, Tho' Satan's darts at   me are hurl'd;
4. I   want to scale the utmost height, And catch a gleam of glo - ry bright;

Still pray-ing as I onward bound, "Lord, plant my feet on higher ground."
Tho' some may dwell where these abound, My pray'r, my aim is higher ground."
For faith has caught the joyful sound, The song of saints on higher ground."
But still I'll pray till heav'n I've found, "Lord, lead me on to higher ground."

CHORUS.

Lord, lift me up   and let me stand, By faith, on heav- en's ta - ble-land;

A high-er plane than I have found, Lord, plant my feet on higher ground.

KEEP ON PRAYING.

R. O. Smith.   J. Lincoln Hall.

1. Soldier, is the battle long? Keep on praying ; Right will surely conquer wrong,
2. Pilgrim, have you weary grown? Keep on praying ; Christ won't leave you all alone,
3. Christian has your faith grown weak? Keep on praying ; Do the tears roll down your cheek?
4. O the joys we'll soon receive, Keep on praying ; If in Christ our hearts believe,

Keep on praying. Do not heed the cannon's roar, Wars shall cease and be no more,
Keep on praying. God will hear your eager pray'r, Soon a starry crown you'll wear,
Keep on praying. Soon you never more will sigh, Tears no more will dim your eye,
Keep on praying. If to Jesus we belong, Soon we'll join the ransom'd throng,

Chorus.

And our Captain's on be-fore, Keep on praying. ⎤
And the joys of heav'n you'll share, Keep on praying. ⎟ Keep on praying,
You will conquer by and by, Keep on praying. ⎟
And we'll sing redemption's song, Keep on praying. ⎦

Keep on praying ; You will conquer by and by, Keep on praying.

HALLELUJAH! JESUS LIVES!

C. A. M.

C. AUSTIN MILES.

1. Tho' the tomb essayed to hold him in its dark embrace, Hallelujah! Je - sus
2. Jesus Christ, the Saviour, liveth in my heart to-day, Halle- lu-jah! Je - sus
3. Ev'ry one who seeks salvation will this grace receive, Halle- lu-jah! Je - sus
4. By and by we'll meet this Jesus, when he claims his own, Hallelujah! Je - sus

lives! In the morning, in the garden, Mary met him face to face, Halle-
lives! Since his pard'ning pow'r has reached me, I've been singing all the way, Halle-
lives! If on Christ, the risen Saviour, in their hearts they will believe, Halle-
lives! And our crowns of vict'ry wearing, we will sing around the throne, Halle-

CHORUS.

lujah! Je - sus lives! Halle - lu - jah! hal - le - lu - jah!
Hallelujah! hallelujah!

We will tell the bless- ed tid- ings o'er and o'er; Hal - le-
o'er and o'er;

lu - jah! hal - le - lu - jah! Je - sus lives for ev - er - more!
Hallelujah! hallelujah!

No. 17. VICTORY THROUGH GRACE.

SALLIE MARTIN.

JNO. R. SWENEY.

1. Conquering now and still to conquer, Rideth a King in his might,
2. Conquering now and still to conquer, Who is this won-der-ful King?
3. Conquering now and still to conquer, Je-sus, thou Rul-er of all,

Leading the host of all the faith-ful In-to the midst of the fight;
Whence are the armies which he lead-eth, While of his glo-ry they sing?
Thrones and their sceptres all shall per-ish, Crowns and their splendor shall fall,

See them with cour-age ad-vanc-ing, Clad in their brilliant ar-ray,
He is our Lord and Re-deem-er, Saviour and mon-arch di-vine,
Yet shall tho arm-ies thou lead-est, Faithful and true to the last,

FINE.

Shouting the name of their Leader, Hear them exult-ing-ly say.
They are the stars that for-ev-er Bright in his kingdom will shine.
Find in thy mansions e-ter-nal Rest, when their warfare is past.

D S.—Yet to the true and the faith-ful Vict'ry is promised through grace.

CHORUS.

D.S.

Not to the strong is the bat-tle, Not to the swift is the race,

No. 18.   SCATTER SUNSHINE.

Lanta Wilson Smith.

E. O. Excell.

1. In a world where sorrow Ev - er will be known Where are found the
2. Slight-est ac-tions oft - en Meet the sor - est needs, For the world wants
3. When the days are gloomy, Sing some hap-py song, Meet the world's re-

need - y, And the sad and lone; How much joy and com - fort
dai - ly, Lit - tle kind - ly deeds; Oh, what care and sor - row,
pin - ing, With a cour - age strong; Go with faith un-daunt - ed,

You can all be - stow, If you scat-ter sunshine Ev-'ry where you go.
You may help re - move, With your songs and courage, Sympathy and love.
Thro' the ills of life, Scatter smiles and sunshine, O'er its toil and strife,

CHORUS.

Scat - - - ter sun-shine all a-long your way,......... Cheer and bless and
Scatter the smiles and   o-ver the way,

1. bright - en Ev - 'ry pass-ing day,
2. Ev - 'ry pass-ing day.

No. 19.   SOME DAY.

J. W. VanDeVenter.   W. S. Weeden.

DUET.

1. Some day, when time shall be no more, When we ap - pear be - fore the
2. Some day our tears will cease to flow, And we shall live and ne'er grow
3. Some day, a - mong the ransom'd throng, Arrayed in robes of spot- less
4. Some day we'll lay our burdens down, And cease our toil to be at

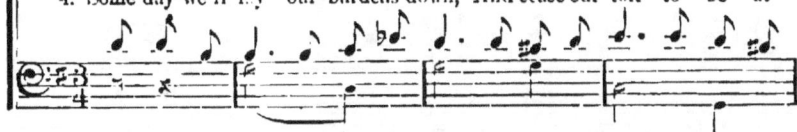

throne, Then all our tri - als will be o'er, And we shall know as we are known.
old ; We'll leave the changing scenes below To view the cit - y built of gold.
white, We'll rise to sing the glad new song Above the gloomy shades of night.
rest ; We'll leave the cross to wear the crown And dwell forev- er with the blest.

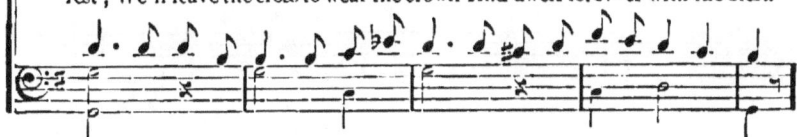

CHORUS.

Some day, we can - not tell just when, But O the joy when Christ shall come !

The saints shall rise to meet him then, And we shall all be gath - ered home.
                                                  shall all   be gathered home.

No. 20. MY SINS ARE ALL TAKEN AWAY.

F. C. B.   F. C. Bilden.

1. He will mention them no more for - ev - er,   My sins are all
2. Since I came by faith to Calv'ry's fount-ain, My sins are all
3. On the bot - tom of the sea they're ly - ing, My sins are all
4. Once the "car-nal mind" was all my pleas - ure, My sins are all
5. Doubt can nev - er stay where faith is sing - ing, My sins are all

tak-en a - way; For his roy - al promise chang-es nev - er,
tak-en a - way; Thro' the cleansing pow'r of that blest fount-ain,
tak-en a - way; Now the pow'rs of sin and self de - ny - ing,
tak-en a - way; God's e - ter - nal word is now my treas - ure,
tak-en a - way; "Praise the Lord" within my heart is ring - ing,

CHORUS.

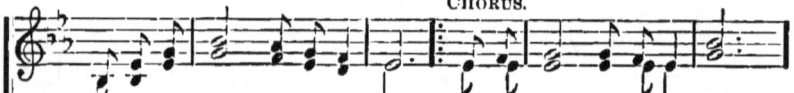

My sins are all taken a - way, They are all tak-en a - way,
a-way,

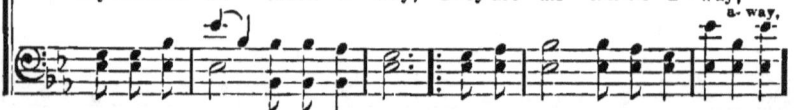

They are all tak-en a - way; He will mention them no more forever,
a-way;

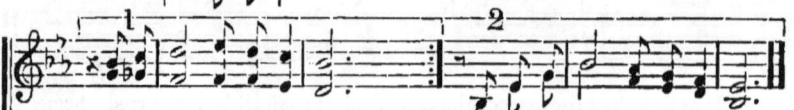

1.   2.

Praise the Lord! sing it to-day,   (Omit.................................)
(Omit...............................) Hal-le-lu-jah! My sins are all tak-en a - way.

No. 21. HIS LOVE CAN SATISFY.

L. E. J.   (DUET, OR QUARTET AND CHORUS.)   L. E. JONES.

1. O troubled heart,............ no long- er sigh,........... The love of
2. O fear- ful heart,............there's peace for thee,.......... The blood ap-
3. O burdened heart,........... find rest from care,........... The Mas- ter

1. O troubled heart,   no longer sigh,

Christ........ can sat- is - fy;............ O come in faith,.......... and lowly
plied......... will set you free ;.......... To Calv'ry's mount.......... for cleansing
waits......... your load to bear ;.......... Let ev- 'ry grief............ to him be

The love of Christ   can sat- is- fy;   O come in faith,

bow,.............. The Lord is here,............ receive him now................
go,................And wash your robes.......... as white as snow................
giv'n,.............And trust his love............ for joy in heav'n.............

and low- ly bow,   The Lord is here,   receive him now.

CHORUS.

His love............ can satis - fy,   His love............ can satis-
His love can fully sat-is- fy, his love can satisfy, His love can fully sat- is- fy, his

fy ;........ He speaketh peace, and sorrows cease, His love can satisfy..........
love can satisfy ;   His love can fully satis- fy, can satisfy.

No. 22. IS THY HEART RIGHT WITH GOD?

E. A. H.   Rev. Elisha A. Hoffman.

1. Have thy affections been nailed to the cross? Is thy heart right with God?
2. Hast thou do-minion o'er self and o'er sin? Is thy heart right with God?
3. Is there no more condem-nation for sin? Is thy heart right with God?
4. Are all thy pow'rs under Je-sus' control? Is thy heart right with God?
5. Art thou now walking in heaven's pure light? Is thy heart right with God?

Dost thou count all things for Jesus but loss? Is thy heart right with God?
O-ver all e-vil without and within? Is thy heart right with God?
Does Je-sus rule in the temple within? Is thy heart right with God?
Does he each moment a-bide in thy soul? Is thy heart right with God?
Is thy soul wearing the garment of white? Is thy heart right with God?

CHORUS.

Is thy heart right with God, Washed in the crim - son flood,

Cleansed and made holy, humble and lowly, Right in the sight of God?..
of God?

No. 23. LET HIM IN.

Rev. J. B. Atchinson.   E. O. Excell.

1. There's a stranger at the door, Let him in,
2. O-pen now to him your heart, Let him in,
3. Hear you now his lov- ing voice? Let him in,
4. Now ad- mit the heavenly Guest, Let him in,
Let the Saviour in, let the Saviour in,

He has been there oft be - fore, Let him in ;
If you wait he will de - part, Let him in ;
Now, O now make him your choice, Let him in ;
He will make for you a feast, Let him in ;
Let the Saviour in, let the Saviour in ;

Let him in ere he is gone, Let him in the Ho - ly One,
Let him in, he is your Friend, He your soul will sure de - fend,
He is standing at the door, Joy to you he will re - store,
He will speak your sins for - giv'n, And when earth ties all are riven,

Jesus Christ, the Father's Son, Let him in.
He will keep you to the end, Let him in.
And his name you will a - dore, Let him in.
He will take you home to heav'n, Let him in.
Let the Saviour in, let the Saviour in,

No. 24.   LOYALTY TO CHRIST.

Dr. E. T. Cassel.   Flora H. Cassel.

1. Up - on the western plain There comes the signal strain, 'Tis loy - al-ty,
2. O hear ye brave the sound That moves the earth around 'Tis loy - al-ty,
3. Come, join our loy - al throng We'll rout the giant wrong, 'Tis loy - al-ty,
4. The strength of youth we lay At Je - sus' feet to - day, 'Tis loy - al-ty,

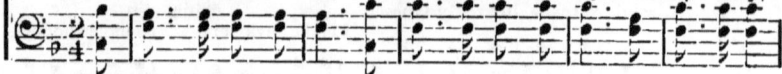

loy - al - ty, loy - al - ty to Christ; Its mu - sic rolls a - long, The
loy - al - ty, loy - al - ty to Christ; A - rise to dare and do, Ring
loy - al - ty, loy - al - ty to Christ; Where Sa - tan's banners float, We'll
loy - al - ty, loy - al - ty to Christ; His gos - pel we'll proclaim, Thro'

FINE.

hills take up the song, Of loy - al - ty, loy - al - ty, Yes, loy - al - ty to Christ.
out the watch-word true, Of loy - al - ty, loy - al - ty, Yes, loy - al - ty to Christ.
send the bu - gle note, Of loy - al - ty, loy - al - ty, Yes, loy - al - ty to Christ.
out the world's domain, Of loy - al - ty, loy - al - ty, Yes, loy - al - ty to Christ.

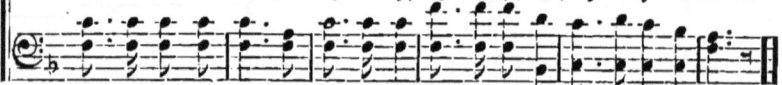

D.S.—Thro' loy - al - ty, loy - al - ty, Yes, loy - al - ty to Christ.

CHORUS.

"On to vic - to - ry! On to vic - to - ry!" Cries our great Commander;

D.S.

"On!" .... We'll move at His command, We'll soon possess the land,
great Commander; "On!"

No. 25. ANYWHERE WITH JESUS.

"I will trust and not be afraid."—Isaiah 12: 2.

Jessie H. Brown.   D. B. Towner.

1. An - y - where with Je - sus I can safe - ly go, An - y - where he
2. An - y - where with Je - sus I am not a - lone, Other friends may
3. An - y - where with Je - sus I can go to sleep, When the darkling

leads me in this world be - low; An - y - where without him, dearest
fail me, he is still my own; Tho' his hand may lead me o - ver
shadows round a - bout me creep; Knowing I shall wak - en, nev - er

joys would fade, An - y - where with Je - sus I am not a - fraid.
drear - est ways, An - y - where with Je - sus is a house of praise.
more to roam, An - y - where with Je - sus will be home, sweet home.

Chorus.

An - y - where! an - y - where! Fear I can - not know;

An - y - where with Je - sus I can safe - ly go.

No. 26.   O HOW LOVE I THY LAW.

"The fear of the Lord is clean, enduring forever."—Ps. 19 : 9.

Anon.

W. S. WEEDEN.

1. Un - spot-ted is the fear of God, And ev - er doth en - dure;
2. They more than gold, yea, much fine gold, To be de - sir - ed are;
3. More - o - ver they, thy serv- ant warn, How he his life should frame;
4. Who can his er - rors un - der-stand? From se - cret faults me cleanse;
5. And do not suf - fer them to have Do - min - ion o - ver me;

The judgments of the Lord are truth, And righteous-ness most pure.
Than hon - ey, hon - ey from the comb That droppeth, sweet - er far.
A great re - ward pro - vid - ed is For them that keep the same.
Thy serv - ant al - so keep thou back From all pre-sumptuous sins.
I shall be right- eous, then, and from The great trans-gres- sion free.

CHORUS.   Psalm 119 : 97.

"O how love I thy law, O how love I thy law; It is my med - i -

ta - tion all........ the day; O how love I thy law, O how

love I thy law; It is my med - i - ta-tion all the day."..........

No. 27. THE VEIL UPLIFTED.

Wm. Kitching, alt.   Chas. H. Gabriel.

1. When the veil shall be up-lift-ed,   Hiding from our mortal sight,
2. When the Saviour home shall call me,   There to taste e-ter-nal joy,
3.   I shall tune my harp with gladness,   While in robes of glo-ry dressed,
4. There, 'midst angels gathered round him,   Strains of heav'nly mu-sic flow;

All that scene of wondrous glo-ry,   Where the saints are robed in white.
Washed in his all-cleansing fountain,   Praise shall be my glad em-ploy.
Round the throne with angels worship,   Sinless and for-ev-er blest.
I shall join th'angel-ic cho-rus,   Such as none on earth may know.

Chorus.

I   shall see what now I   see   not,   Hear what
I shall see what now,   shall   see what now I   see   not,

none   on earth may   hear;............ Walk   in ev-er-lasting
Hear what none on earth,hear what none on earth may hear; Walk in everlast-ing,

sun-shine,   With my Sav - iour ev-er   near............
ev-er-lasting sunshine,   With my Saviour near, my   Saviour ever near.

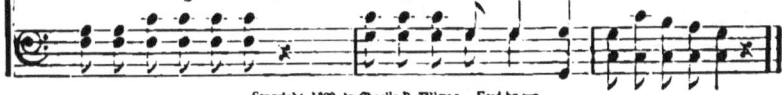

No. 28. "WHAT ARE THEY AMONG SO MANY?"

FLORA KIRKLAND.   John 6: 9.   WM. W. COE.
SOPRANO AND ALTO DUET.

1. Crowds around   the Master gathered, E - ven-tide was drawing nigh ;
2. Crowds to- day   are fainting, starving, Hung'ring for the Living Bread;
3. Take to him your loaves and fish-es,   E - ven tho' they're small and few ;
4. Take your tal - ents and your ef- forts, Take your money, thought and time ;

Five small loaves and two small fish - es Must their need sup - ply.
Who will spread the feast be - fore them That they may   be   fed ?
He   is wait - ing to dis - trib - ute, Waiting now for you.
He will, from your hum- ble off'r - ing, Make a feast   sub - lime.

CHORUS.

"What are they   a - mong so ma - ny?" Ah, but Christ, the Lord, is near ;

He will mul - ti - ply, if need be ; Thou needst nev - er   fear.

No. 29. IN A LITTLE WHILE WE'RE GOING HOME.

E. E. H.   E. E. Hewitt.

1. Let us sing a song that will cheer us by the way, In a little while we're
2. We will do the work that our hands may find to do, In a little while we're
3. We will smooth the path for some weary, wayworn feet, In a little while we're
4. There's a rest beyond, there's relief from ev'ry care, In a little while we're

go - ing home; For the night will end in the ev - er- lasting day, In a
go - ing home; And the grace of God will our daily strength renew, In a
go - ing home; O may loving hearts spread around an influence sweet ! In a
go - ing home; And no tears shall fall in that cit- y bright and fair, In a

CHORUS.

lit- tle while we're go - ing home.   In a   lit - tle while,   In a
                                      In a   lit- tle while,

lit- tle while,   We shall cross the billow's foam ;   We shall meet at last,
In a lit- tle while,

When the stormy winds are past, In a   lit- tle while we're go- ing home.

FOR YOU AND FOR ME.

W. L. T.

WILL. L. THOMPSON.

Very slow.

1. Soft-ly and ten-der-ly Je-sus is calling,—Calling for you and for
2. Why should we tar-ry when Je-sus is pleading,—Pleading for you and for
3. Time is now fleeting, the moments are passing,—Passing from you and from
4. O, for the wonder-ful love he has promised,—Promised for you and for

me. See on the por-tals he's wait-ing and watching,—
me? Why should we lin-ger and heed not his mercies,—
me. Shad-ows are gath-er-ing, death-beds are com-ing,—
me. Though we have sinned he has mer-cy and par-don,—

REFRAIN.

Watching for you and for me. Come home,... come home,.....
Mercies for you and for me?
Com-ing for you and for me.   Come home,   come home
Par-don for you and for me.

cres.   *rit.*   *p*   *pp*

Ye who are wea-ry, come home,......   Ear-nest-ly, ten-der-ly

rit.   *pp*

Je-sus is call-ing,—Call-ing, O sin-ner, come home!

No. 31. HAPPY IN THE LOVE OF JESUS.

JENNIE WILSON. J. LINCOLN HALL.

1. Home to Zi - on we are bound, Hap-py in the love of Je - sus,
2. Trust-ing we will for-ward go, Hap-py in the love of Je - sus,
3. We will sing sal - va-tion's song, Hap-py in the love of Je - sus,
4. Soon we'll reach the home-land fair, Hap-py in the love of Je - sus,

Peace a - bid - ing we have found, Hap-py in the love of Je - sus.
Tread-ing changeful paths be - low, Hap-py in the love of Je - sus.
All our earth - ly way a - long, Hap-py in the love of Je - sus.
And shall dwell for - ev - er there, Hap-py in the love of Je - sus.

CHORUS.

Hap - py, hap - py, Sing-ing all the way, Hap-py all the day;

Hap - py, hap - py, Hap - py in the love of Je - sus.

No. 32.   MY MOTHER'S BIBLE.

M. B. WILLIAMS.

C. D. TILLMAN.

DUET.

1. There's a dear and pre-cious book, Tho' it's worn and faded now, Which re-
2. There she read of Je - sus' love, As he blest the chil-dren dear, How he
3. Well, those days are past and gone, But their mem'ry lin-gers still, And the

calls the hap - py days of long a - go; When I stood at mother's knee,
suf-fered, bled and died up - on the tree; Of his heavy load of care,
dear old Book each day has been my guide; And I seek to do his will,

With her hand up-on my brow, And I heard her voice in gentle tones and low.
Then she dried my flowing tear With her kisses as she said it was for me.
As my mother taught me then, And ev - er in my heart his words abide.

FINE.

D.S.—As I walk the narrow way That leads at last to that bright home above.

CHORUS.

Blessed book,.......... precious book,.......... On thy dear old tear-stained

Bless-ed book,   precious book,

leaves I love to look ;.............. Thou art sweet-er day by day,

love to look ;

D.S.

No. 33. SHOWERS OF BLESSING.

"And I will cause the shower to come down in his season."—Ezekiel 34 : 26.

JENNIE GARNETT.   JNO. R. SWENEY.

1. Here in thy name we are gathered, Come and re-vive us, O Lord;
2. O that the showers of bless-ing Now on our souls may descend,
3. There shall be showers of bless-ing,—Promise that nev-er can fail;
4. Showers of blessing,—we need them, Showers of bless-ing from thee;

"There shall be showers of bless-ing" Thou hast declared in thy word.
While at the footstool of mer-cy Pleading thy prom-ise we bend!
Thou wilt re-gard our pe-ti-tion; Sure-ly our faith will pre-vail.
Showers of bless-ing,—oh, grant them; Thine all the glory shall be.

CHORUS.

Oh! gracious-ly hear us, Gracious-ly hear us, we pray:
gracious-ly hear us,

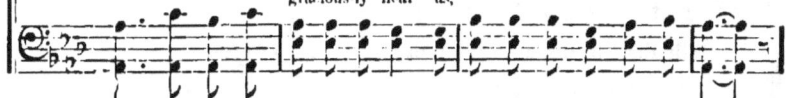

Pour from thy windows up-on us Showers of blessing to-day.
Lord, pour up-on us

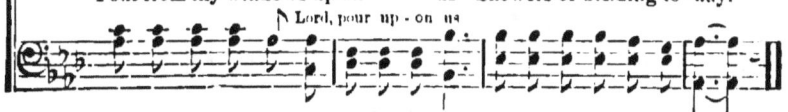

No. 34. WILT THOU BE MADE WHOLE?

W. J. K.

WM. J. KIRKPATRICK.

1. Hear the footsteps of Je-sus, He is now passing by, Bearing balm for the
2. 'Tis the voice of that Saviour, Whose mer-ci-ful call Freely of-fers sal-
3. Are you halting and struggling, O'erpow'red by your sin, While the waters are
4. Blessed Saviour, as-sist us To rest on thy Word; Let the soul-healing

wounded, Healing all who ap-ply; As he spake to the suff'rer Who
va-tion To one and to all; He is now beck'ning to him Each
troubled, Can you not en-ter in? Lo, the Saviour stands waiting To
pow-er On us now be outpoured: Wash a-way ev-'ry sin-spot, Take

S: *Fine.*

lay at the pool, He is say-ing this moment, "Wilt thou be made whole?"
sin-taint-ed soul, And lov-ing-ly asking, "Wilt thou be made whole?"
strengthen your soul, He is earn-est-ly pleading, "Wilt thou be made whole?"
per-fect con-trol, Say to each trusting spirit, "Thy faith makes thee whole."

D. S.—cleansing waves roll: Step in-to the cur-rent and thou shalt be whole.

CHORUS.

Wilt thou be made whole? Wilt thou be made whole? O come, wea-ry

D.S.

suf-f'rer, O come, sin-sick soul; See, the life-stream is flow-ing, See, the

No. 35. THE STORY THAT NEVER GROWS OLD.

John H. Yates.   M. L. McPhail.

1. How dear to my heart is the sto - ry of old, The sto - ry that
2. It came to my heart when, all fet-tered by sin, I sat in the
3. It comes to my soul when the tempter is nigh With snares for my
4. When sor-row is mine, and on pil-lows of stone My ach - ing head
5. When down in the "val-ley and shad-ow of Death," I en - ter the

ev - er is new, The mes-sage that saints of all a - ges have told,
pris - on of doubt: Like an - gel of old, the glad sto - ry came in
way-wea - ry - feet; It tells of the Rock that is high - er than I,
seeks for re - pose, This sto - ry brings comfort and peace from the throne,
gloom of the grave, I'll tell the old sto - ry with life's lat - est breath

CHORUS.

The mes-sage so ten - der and true.)
And led me tri - umphant - ly out.)
And leads to its bliss-ful re - treat.)   The sto - ry that nev - er grows
My des - ert blooms forth like the rose.)   that
Of Christ and his pow - er to save.)

old, ... Though o - ver and o - ver 'tis told : .... The
nev - er grows old,   'tis told :

sto - ry so dear, bringing heav'n so near, Sweet sto-ry that nev - er grows old.

No. 36. THE HEAVENLY SUMMERLAND.

ALICE JEAN CLEATOR.   J. LINCOLN HALL.

1. Be-yond the winter's storm and blight, Beyond the summer's shining strand,
2. No ling'ring shad-ow of the night, Shall dim the glo - ry of that shore;
3. No part-ing word, no tears nor pain, Shall pass those portals fair and bright,

There waits a land of joy and light—O bright and fadeless summer-land!
There all is joy and song and light, And rest and peace for-ev - er - more!
There part-ed friends shall meet again, With-in that Land of love and light!

CHORUS.

O summer-land......... that gleams a-far,......... Beyond the light........
O summerland   that gleams afar   beyond the light

of sun or star,........... O sum-mer - land,......... O sum-mer-
of sun or star,   O summerland,

land......... we long for thee,   dear sum-merland.
O summerland,   thee, we long for thee,   dear summerland.

ONWARD! FORWARD!

With Spirit.

Words and Music by Rev. W. W. Coe.

1. On- ward! forward! Sol-diers of En-deav - or, Christ, our Mas - ter
2. Foes may threaten, storms may gather round us, And the way seem
3. Forward, comrades, Christ the Lord hath spok-en, "As thy days are,
4. Rouse then, Christians, Soldiers of En-deav - or, Fol - low where our

giv - eth the com-mand, Gird your ar-mor, follow where He leads you Till His
dark and lone and drear, But our faith shall nev-er fail or fal - ter With our
so thy strength shall be," Halt not, doubt not, neither stand ye i - dle While the
Captain leads the way, Till at last He leads us in - to glory Where we'll

CHORUS.

name is known in ev - 'ry land.
Saviour's liv-ing presence near.
Mas - ter calls to vic - to - ry.
reign with Him thro' endless day.

Let us fight for the right,

Let us fight for the right,

For Christ has promised, be it known, To sus-tain for-
Christ has promised

ev - er ev-'ry true be - liev-er, And we'll trust Him till the vict'ry's won.

No. 38. HAVE FAITH IN GOD.

E. E. HEWITT.
DUET.
GEO. F. ROSCHE.

1. "Have faith in God," the Saviour said; He saw the path that we must tread;
2. Have faith in God tho' clouds a-rise And o-ver-spread the glowing skies;
3. Have faith in God: A father's heart Would to his child all good im-part;
4. Have faith in God: his word di-vine By day and night shall brightly shine,

The frequent thorn, the fading flow'r, The joy or pain of ev-'ry hour.
Tho' sun and stars grow dim and pale, His boundless love shall never fail.
Much more will he   re-gard the pray'r Of those who cast on him their care.
Un - til we pass the gates of light And faith shall yield to bliss-ful sight.

CHORUS. *Faster.*

O bless - ed faith!   Its song of cheer   Re-vives our
            O faith !   of cheer
The Shep-herd's staff,   The Shepherd's rod,   (Omit............
            the staff,   the rod,

hope,   dispels our fear;
    our hope,   our fear;
....) Still leads us on; have faith in God.
                                                        in God.

No. 39. HOLY SPIRIT DWELL IN ME.

Respectfully Dedicated to Winona Bible Conference.

E. S. B.

E. S. BLACK.

1. Ho - ly Spir - it dwell in me, Teach mine err - ing feet the way;
2. Ho - ly Spir - it dwell in me, Fill my soul with thy rich grace;
3. Ho - ly Spir - it dwell in me, Till life's night has passed a - way;

As I jour - ney here be - low, Guide me ev - 'ry day.
Let me all the beau - ty see, In my Sav - iour's face.
When with rap - ture I shall wake In e - ter - nal day.

Show me what I ought to do, Help me shun the wrong,
Till at last his life shall be Mir - rored in mine own,
I shall dwell with Christ my Lord In our heav'n - ly home,

In this va - ried chain of life Make the weak link strong.
And the like - ness God can see, To his own dear Son.
And he will pre - sent me then, Fault - less at the throne.

SAY! WILL YOU MEET ME THERE?

MAY MAURICE.   WM. J. KIRKPATRICK.

1. When my wea - ry feet reach the shin - ing goal, And the Master's
2. When I sweet - ly rest on that peace- ful shore, Where the blight of
3. When I stand at last with the white-robed throng, To a- dore my

voice greets my raptured soul; Where the waves of joy shall around me roll,
sin shall be felt no more; When I find the loved ones who've gone before,
King, and his praise prolong; When my voice shall join in the glad, new song,

CHORUS.

O say, will you meet me there? Say, will you
O say,

meet me there? Say, will you meet me there? In the home a-
O say,

bore, in the land of love, O say, will you meet me there?

ABIDE IN ME.

P. K.

Flora Kirkland.

1. O, to what "wondrous one-ness"   Calleth the Lord to-day!
2. On-ly by rep-e-ti-tion   Lit-tle ones learn to read;
3. List-ening, Lord, to hear thee,   Thinking of what we hear;
4. Seeking to know thee ful-ly,   Giv-ing the need-ful time;

Quicken our com-pre-hen-sion, Help us "a-bide," we pray.
O-ver the same slow path-way, Je-sus his own would lead.
Praying in full sur-ren-der, Grasping thy meaning clear.
Yielding our be-ings *whol-ly*, Waiting thy touch di-vine.

REFRAIN.

Day aft-er day spell o-ver Simply, "A-bide in me;"

Day aft-er day dis-cov-er What Je-sus meant for thee.

No. 42.   IN THY NAME WE GATHER.

J. B. M.

J. B. MACKAY.

1. In thy name we gather, gracious Lord divine, May thy love most tender
2. Bod - y, soul and spirit, Lord, we give to thee, Thine, yea, thine alone for-
3. Fit us for thy service, teach us all thy will, Ev - 'ry precious promise
4. Je - sus, blessed Saviour, when we meet at last In the land where partings

'round our hearts entwine; Guide us by thy Spir - it, lead us in thy way,
ev - ermore to be; Heaven's rich - est blessing now on us be- stow
now in us ful - fill; Help us tell the sto - ry of thy wondrous name
are for - ev - er past, Saved by grace di - vine to all e - ter - ni - ty,

CHORUS.

Meet, O meet with us to - day.   Meet.......... with us, dear
Till our hearts shall o - ver - flow.
Till it set the world a - flame.
We will give the praise to thee.

Meet with us dear Sav- iour,

Sav - iour,   Meet.......... with us we pray;
meet with us to-day,   O meet,   pray, with us we pray;

In thy ho - ly name we gath - er, O meet.... with us to - day.
Saviour, meet   to-day.

No. 43. MY MOTHER'S PRAYER.

J. W. Van De Venter. W. S. Weeden.

1. I nev-er can for-get the day I heard my moth-er kind-ly say,
2. I nev-er can for-get the voice That always made my heart re-joice;
3. Tho' years have gone, I can't forget Those words of love—I hear them yet;
4. I nev-er can for-get the hour I felt the Saviour's cleansing pow'r,

" You're leaving now my tender care; Remember, child, your mother's pray'r."
Tho' I have wandered God knows where, Still I remember mother's pray'r.
I see her by the old arm chair, My mother dear, in humble pray'r.
My sin and guilt he canceled there, 'Twas there he answered mother's pray'r.

CHORUS.

1, 2, & 3. Whene'er I think of her so dear, I feel her an - gel spir - it near;
4. Oh, praise the Lord for sav- ing grace! We'll meet up yonder face to face

A voice comes floating on the air, Reminding me of mother's pray'r.
The home a-bove to-geth-er share, In an-swer to my mother's pray'r.

No. 44.   I MUST TELL JESUS.

E. A. H.

Rev. Elisha A. Hoffman.

1. I must tell Je - sus all of my tri - als; I can-not bear these
2. I must tell Je - sus all of my troub - les; He is a kind, com -
3. Tempted and tried I need a great Sav - ior, One who can help my
4. O how the world to e - vil al - lures me! O how my heart is

burdens a - lone; In my dis-tress he kind-ly will help me; He ev - er
passionate Friend; If I but ask him, he will de - liv - er, Make of my
burdens to bear; I must tell Je - sus, I must tell Je - sus; He all my
tempted to sin! I must tell Je - sus, And he will help me O - ver the

loves and cares for his own.
troub - les quick-ly an end.
cares and sor-rows will share.
world the vic-t'ry to win.

Chorus.

I must tell Je - sus! I must tell Je - sus! I can-not bear my bur-dens a - lone; I must tell Je - sus! I must tell Je - sus! Je-sus can help me, Je-sus a - lone.

Rit.

No. 45. THERE IS POWER IN THE BLOOD.

L. E. J.

L. E. JONES.

1. Would you be free from your bur-den of sin? There's pow'r in the blood,
2. Would you be free from your passion and pride? There's pow'r in the blood,
3. Would you be whit-er, much whiter than snow? There's pow'r in the blood,
4. Would you do serv-ice for Jesus your King? There's pow'r in the blood,

pow'r in the blood; Would you o'er e-vil a vic-to-ry win?
pow'r in the blood; Come for a cleans-ing to Cal-va-ry's tide,
pow'r in the blood; Sin stains are lost in its life-giv-ing flow,
pow'r in the blood; Would you live dai-ly his prais-es to sing?

Chorus.

There's won-der-ful pow'r in the blood. There is pow'r, pow'r,

There is pow'r,

wonder-working pow'r In the blood of the Lamb; There is

In the blood of the Lamb;

pow'r, pow'r, wonder-working pow'r In the precious blood of the Lamb.

There is pow'r,

No. 46.   **THE BETTER LAND.**

"A better country, that is an heavenly."—Heb. 11 : 16.

Gurdon Robins, arr.   Daniel B. Towner.

1. There is a land mine eye hath seen In visions of enraptured thought,
2. A land up - on whose blissful shore There rests no shad-ow, falls no stain ;
3. Its skies are not like earth-ly skies, With va-rying hues of shade and light ;
4. There sweeps no des-o - la - ting wind A-cross the calm, se-rene a - bode.

So bright, that all which spreads between Is with its ra-diant glo - ries fraught.
There those who meet shall part no more, And those long parted meet a - gain.
It hath no need of suns, to rise To dis - si- pate the gloom of night.
The wand'rer there a home may find Within the par - a - dise of God.

CHORUS.

Oh, land of love,...... of joy and light,...... Thy glo-ries

Oh, land of love,   of joy and light,

gild........ earth's darkest night; Thy tranquil shore,...

Thy glories gild earth's darkest night (earth's darkest night ;)   Thy tranquil shore,

we, too, shall see,...... When day shall break.... and shadows flee.

(we, too, shall see,)   When day shall break

No. 47. SINGING ON THE WAY.

W. H. B.

W. H. BROWN.

1. On the good old road that our fathers trod, Singing on the way, halle-
2. Tho' temptations come I will trust the Lord, Singing on the way, halle-
3. I will meet the friends who have gone before, Singing on the way, halle-
4. It will not be long if my faith be strong, Singing on the way, halle-

lu - jah! To a cit - y whose build - er and mak - er is God,
lu - jah! "Be of cheer," Je - sus said, and I trust in his word,
lu - jah! In that bright, summer land where we'll part nev - er-more,
lu - jah! When I'll join in the song of the heav - en - ly throng,

CHORUS.

Singing on the way, hal - lo - lu - jah! Praise the Lord, what a

joy is mine! Hal - le - lu- jah, I've a peace di - vine! 'Round my

heart doth his love entwine, Singing on the way, hal - le - lu - jah!

No. 48. SCATTER SUNSHINE BY THE WAY.

Eben E. Rexford.   Chas. H. Gabriel.

1. Do you know a heart that hungers For a word of love and cheer?
2. It may be that some one fal-ters On the brink of sin and wrong,
3. Nev-er think kind deeds are wasted, Bread up-on the waves are they,

There are ma-ny, you may find them In the byways far and near; And to
Just a word from you might save him, Make the falt'ring brother strong; Then be
And the tides of God may bring them Back to us, some coming day, Back to

weak, discourag'd comrades Speak the word that's needed so, And your own heart will be
earnest! look about you! What a sin is yours and mine, If we see that help is
us when sorely needed, In a time of sharp distress, So let's do them gladly,

CHORUS.

strengthen'd By the help that you bestow.) Would you doub - - le all the
needed, And we give no friendly sign. }
knowing Gift and giver God will bless.) Would you doub - le,

bless - ings,   As they come......... from day to day?   Go and
double all the blessings,   As they come from   day to day?

SCATTER SUNSHINE BY THE WAY.—Concluded.

share....... them with anoth - er,   Scatter sunshine by the way.
Go and share them, share them with another,

No. 49.   WILL JESUS FIND US WATCHING?

Fanny J. Crosby.   W. H. Doane.

1. When Jesus comes to reward his servants, Whether it be noon or night,
2. If at the dawn of the ear- ly morning, He shall call us one by one,
3. Have we been true to the trust he left us? Do we seek to do our best?
4. Blessed are those whom the Lord finds watching, In his glory they shall share;

ril.

Faithful to him will he find us watching, With our lamps all trimm'd and bright.
When to the Lord we restore our talents, Will he answer thee— Well done?
If in our hearts there is naught condemns us, We shall have a glorious rest.
If he shall come at the dawn or midnight, Will he find us watching there?

Chorus.

O, can we say we are ready, brother? Ready for the soul's bright home?

Say, will he find you and me still watching, Waiting, waiting when the Lord shall come?

No. 50. I WANT TO GO THERE.

Words and Melody by D. Sullins. Harmony by Prof. Riggs. C. F. College.

1. They tell of a cit-y far up in the sky, I want to go
2. Its gates are all pearl, its streets are all gold, I want to go
3. When the old ship of Zi-on shall make her last trip, I want to be
4. When Je-sus is crowned the King of all kings, I want to be

there, I do; 'Tis built in the land of "the sweet by and by,"
there, I do; The Lamb is the light of that cit-y we're told,
there, I do; With heads all un-cov-ered to greet the old ship,
there, I do; With shout-ing and clap-ping till all heav-en rings,

I want to go there, don't you? There Je-sus has gone to pre-
I want to go there, don't you? Death robs us all here, there
I want to be there, don't you? When all the ship's com-pany
I want to be there, don't you? Hal-le-lu-jah! we'll shout a-

pare us all homes, I want to go there, I do; Where sick-ness nor
none ev-er die, I want to go there, I do; There loved ones will
meet on the strand, I want to be there, I do; With songs on their
gain and a-gain, I want to be there, I do; And close with the

sor-row nor death ev-er comes, I want to go there, don't you?
nev-er a-gain say good-bye, I want to go there, don't you?
lips and with harps in their hands, I want to be there, don't you?
cho-rus, A-men and A-men, I want to be there, don't you?

I WANT TO GO THERE. -Concluded.

CHORUS.

1. 2. I want to go there, I want to go there, I want to go there, I do;
3. 4. I want to be there, I mean to be there, I ex-pect to be there, I do;

I want to go there, I want to go there, I want to go there, don't you?
I want to be there, I mean to be there, I ex-pect to be there, don't you?

No. 51. NEARER, STILL NEARER.

C. H. M.

Mrs. C. H. Morris.

1. Near - er, still near - er, close to thy heart, Draw me, my Sav-iour, so
2. Near - er, still near - er, noth-ing I bring, Naught as an off-'ring to
3. Near - er, still near - er, Lord, to be thine Sin, with its fol - lies, I
4. Near - er, still near - er, while life shall last, Till all its strug-gles and

precious thou art; Fold me, O fold me close to thy breast, Shelter me
Je - sus my King; On - ly my sin - ful, now contrite heart. Grant me the
glad-ly re - sign; All of its pleasures, pomp and its pride. Give me but
tri - als are past; Then thro' e - ternity, ev - er I'll be Near er, my

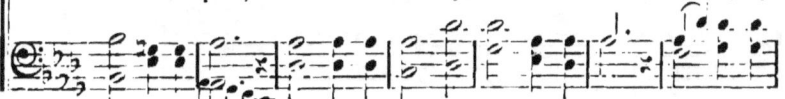

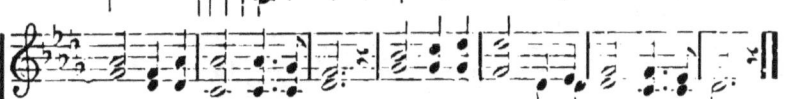

safe in that "Haven of Rest," Shelter me safe in that "Haven of Rest."
cleansing thy blood doth impart, Grant me the cleansing thy blood doth impart.
Je - sus, my Lord cruci - fied, Give me but Je-sus, my Lord cruci - fied.
Saviour, still nearer to thee, Near-er, my Sav-iour, still nearer so thee.

No. 52. THE MASTER'S CALL.

Geo. I. Runion.

Chas. H. Gabriel.

1. Hark! I hear the Saviour call- ing from a - cross the rag- ing flood,
2. Hark! I hear the Saviour call- ing, "will you not go forth to - day,
3. Hark! I hear the Saviour call-ing, let your light shine bright and clear;

"Child of mine, go forth to rescue those I've purchased with my blood; Time is
Help some weary, sin-sick wand'rer find the bright and narrow way? Tell him
In a world of sin and sorrow scatter gladness far and near; Tell to

flying, souls are dying, hasten then to bring them in ; Do not rest while struggling
there is peace and comfort, happiness and joy complete, If he'll come, his sin con-
sinners all about you Christ has died to set them free, Tell them Je- sus lives to

Chorus.

brothers sink beneath the weight of sin." ⎱
fessing, kneeling at the mercy seat." ⎰   Brother, heed.............. the urgent
save them from their sins and misery." ⎰   Brother, heed the urgent call, O

call,............ There is work........... for one and all ;............. Do not
heed the urgent call, There is work for one and all, there is work for one and all;

THE MASTER'S CALL.—Concluded.

lay the armor down 'Till you're won the golden crown,' Till you're won the golden crown.

No. 53. SINCE I FOUND MY SAVIOUR.

(MAY BE USED AS A SOLO AND CHORUS.)

E. E. HEWITT.   JNO. R. SWENEY.

1. Life wears a dif - ferent face to me,   Since I found my Sav-iour;
2. He sought me in   his wondrous love,   So   I found my Sav-iour,
3. The pass-ing clouds may in - ter- vene, Since I found my Sav-iour,
4. A strong hand kindly holds my own,   Since I found my Sav-iour,

Rich mer - cy at   the   cross I see,   My dy - ing, liv - ing Sav-iour.
He brought salva- tion from a- bove,   My dear, almight - y Sav- iour.
But he is with me, though unseen,   My ev - er-pres - ent Sav- iour.
It leads me on - ward to the throne, O there I'll see my Sav- iour.

CHORUS.

Gold-en sunbeams 'round me play,   Je - sus turns my night to   day,

Heav - en seems not   far   a- way,   Since I found my   Sav - iour.

No. 54.
J. W. H.

THE SAVIOUR CALLS.

SOLO, OR DUETT. Dedicated to W. S. Weeden. J. WESLEY HUGHES.

Tenderly.

1. The Saviour calls, He calls for thee; List' to His lov - ing accents
2. He calls thee from Geth-sem - a - ne, In lone - ly sor - row bend-ing
3. He calls a - gain from Cal - va - ry, Oh, hath He died for thee in

sweet. O hear Him say "come un - to me," And thou shalt find a joy com -
low; O see Him there in ag - o - ny! For thee the bloody sweat-drops
vain; He bore thy sins up - on the tree, And wilt thou nail Him there a-

SOLO.

plete. O tar - ry not while Je - sus waits! All thy transgressions He'll for-
flow. He calls thee by His pier- ced brow, He calls thee by His wounded
gain. He calls thee by His dy - ing love! He calls thee to thy heav'nly

DUETT.

give. And an-gels near the golden gates Now bid thee turn to Christ and live.
side: How canst thou slight His mercy now, For thee, for thee the Saviour died.
home. He calls in mer - cy from a-bove, This way, my child, no long-er roam.

CHO. OR QUAR.

The Sav - iour calls, O sin - ner, come home!............

The Sav - iour calls, O si.....

THE SAVIOUR CALLS.—Concluded.

The Sav - iour calls, why lon - ger roam?...... cast - ing thy

The Sav - iour calls, why lon - ger roam?

Rall.

soul at Je - sus feet, Thou shalt find a par - don sweet.

No. 55. REST FOR THE WEARY.

Rev S. G. Harmer.   Rev. W. McDonald.

1. { In the Christian's home in glo - ry, There re-mains a land of rest:
     There my Saviour's gone be - fore me, (*Omit*......................)

2. { Pain nor sickness ne'er shall en - ter, Grief nor woe my lot shall share;
     But in that ce - les - tial cen - tre, (*Omit*......................)

3. { Sing, oh, sing, ye heirs of glo - ry; Shout your tri-umphs as you go;
     Zi - on's gates will o - pen for you, (*Omit*......................)

To ful - fill my soul's request.)
I a crown of life shall wear. }
You shall find an entrance thro'.)

CHORUS.

{ There is rest for the wea-ry, There is
{ On the oth - er side of Jor-dan, In the

rest for the wea-ry, There is rest for the weary, There is rest for you— }
sweet fields of Eden, Where the tree of life is blooming, There is rest for you. }

No. 56. EVERYTHING, YES, EVERYTHING.

J. W. Van De Venter.   W. S. Weeden.

1. All my sins I bring to Je-sus, Ev-'ry bur-den of my soul.
2. All my heart I bring to Je-sus, Ev-'ry tal-ent I pos-sess.
3. All my life I bring to Je-sus, Ev-'ry mo-ment, ev-'ry hour.
4. All my plans I bring to Je-sus, All am-bi-tions I re-sign.
5. All I have I bring to Je-sus, All I am, and hope to be;

I am stand-ing on the prom-ise, And I know, He makes me whole.
Trust-ing on-ly in His mer-it, "Je-sus blood and righteous-ness.
All I have is on the al-tar, And He fills me with His pow'r.
Emp-tied for the Ho-ly Spir-it, "I am His, and He is mine.
Ev-'ry thing is His for-ev-er, His for all e-ter-ni-ty.

Chorus.

Ev-'ry-thing, yes, ev-'ry-thing, All I lay at Je-sus' feet,

Ev-'ry-thing, yes, ev-'ry-thing, "For the Master's use made meet."

No. 57. CONSECRATION.

Chas. A. Ford. J. A. Birkholz.

1. Set a - part for spe-cial du - ty, From the world and self and sin,
2. Yielding up, with joy and gladness, Worldly pleasures that of - fend
3. This then be my con- se - cra- tion; This my sep - a - ration be:

To the serv - ice of our mas - ter, With the bat - tle-field within;
Those who are our weak- er breth- ren, Making less their heav'nly trend;
That thy will be my will ev - er, Fill'd my life with on - ly thee;

'Tis no form - al sep - a - ra - tion That with joy and peace doth fill,
Will- ing that for Christ, my Sav- iour, To be naught or less, if need,
This my peace now, as a riv - er, Flowing broad - ly on and deep,

Fine.

But the will - ing sub - ju - ga - tion Of our own un - fettered will.
If he may be all and in all, And be giv'n his roy - al meed.
Till my Lord, who is the giv - er, Giv-eth his be - lov - ed sleep.

D. S.—serv - ice of our Mas - ter, Helping him the world to win.

Chorus. *D. S.*

Con- se- cra- ted, sep - a - ra - ted From our love of self and sin To the

No. 58. WHEN YOU HAVE FOUND THE SAVIOUR.

IDA L. REED.

LEWIS S. CHAFER.

DUET.

1. When you have found the Sav-iour, And peace thro' him have known,
2. Lead oth-er souls to Je-sus, He who your sins for-gave,
3 Go, bear the bless-ed ti-dings, Of his sal-va-tion free,
4. Go, tell when you have found him, How gra-cious and how kind

Then straightway seek your broth-er, And lead him to the throne.
Whose love you've found so pre-cious, And tell them he will save.
To all who may not know him, That they redeemed may be.
Is Je-sus your Re-deem-er, And help them him to find.

CHORUS.

When you have found the Sav-iour, Go forth and glad-ly tell

The joy-ful news to oth-ers, That they his praise may swell.

No. 59. LEAD ME GENTLY HOME, FATHER.

W. L. T.

W. L. Thompson.

Use as Solo or Duett.

1. Lead me gen-tly home, Father, Lead me gently home, When life's toils are
2. Lead me gen-tly home, Father, Lead me gently home, In life's darkest

end - ed, And part - ing days have come, Sin no more shall tempt me,
hours, Fa-ther, When life's troubles come, Keep my feet from wand'ring,

rit. *p*

Ne'er from thee I'll roam, If thou'lt only lead me, Father, Lead me gently home.
Lest from thee I roam, Lest I fall up-on the wayside, Lead me gently home.

CHORUS.

Lead me gen-tly home, Fa-ther, Lead me gen-tly,

Lead me gen-tly home, Fa-ther, Lead me gen-tly home, Fa-ther,

Lest I fall up-on the way-side, Lead me gen-tly home,
Lead me gen-tly, gen-tly home.

No. 60.　　　　BEAUTIFUL ROBES.

E. E. Hewitt.　　　　　　　　　　　　　Wm. J. Kirkpatrick.

Not too fast.

1. We shall walk with him in white, In that coun - try pure and bright,
2. We shall walk with him in white, Where faith yields to bliss - ful sight,
3. We shall walk with him in white, By the fount - ains of de - light,

Where shall enter naught that may de-file; Where the day-beam ne'er declines,
When the beau - ty of the King we see; Hold-ing converse full and sweet,
Where the Lamb his ransomed ones shall lead; For his blood shall wash each stain,

For the bless-ed light that shines Is the glo - ry of the Saviour's smile.
In a fel - low-ship complete; Waking songs of ho - ly mel - o - dy.
Till no spot of sin re-main, And the soul for-ev - er-more is freed.

Chorus.

Beau - - ti - ful robes,......... Beau - - ti - ful robes,......

Beau-ti - ful robes, beau-ti - ful robes, Beau-ti-ful robes, beau-ti - ful robes,

Beau - ti - ful robes we then shall wear,.....

Beau-ti - ful robes we then shall wear, Beau-ti - ful robes we then shall wear,

BEAUTIFUL ROBES.—Concluded.

Gar - - ments of light,........ Love - ly and bright,......
Garments of light, garments of light, Love-ly and bright, love-ly and bright,

Walk-ing with Je - sus in white, Beau - ti - ful robes we shall wear.

No. 61. THOU THINKEST, LORD, OF ME.

"The Lord thinkest upon me."—Ps. 11 : 17.

E. D. Mund.   E. S. Lorenz.

1. A - mid the tri - als which I meet, Amid the thorns that pierce my feet,
2. The cares of life come thronging fast, Up - on my soul their shad-ow cast;
3. Let shadows come, let shadows go, Let life be bright or dark with woe,

FINE.

One thought remains su-preme-ly sweet, Thou thinkest, Lord, of me!
Their gloom re-minds my heart at last, Thou thinkest, Lord, of me!
I am con-tent for this I know, Thou thinkest, Lord, of me!

D.S.—What need I fear since thou art near, And thinkest, Lord, of me!

CHORUS.   D.S.

Thou think-est, Lord, of me, Thou thinkest, Lord, of me!
of me, of me!

Copyright of E. S. Lorenz. By per.

No. 62. JESUS SAVES ME ALL THE TIME.

W. S. W.   J. MOUNTAIN.

Smoothly.

1. Je - sus saves me ev - 'ry day, Je - sus saves me ev - 'ry night,
2. Je - sus saves, can I re - pine? Je - sus saves when I re - joice;
3. Je - sus saves when sorrows come, Je - sus saves when death appears;
4. Je - sus saves me, he is mine; Je - sus saves me, I am his;

Je - sus saves me all the way, Thro' the dark- ness, thro' the light.
Je - sus saves when hopes de- cline—Faith can al - ways hear his voice.
Je - sus saves and leads me home, How he saves from doubts and fears.
Je - sus saves as I re - cline On his pre - cious prom- is - es.

CHORUS.

Je- sus saves, O mighty pow'r! Jesus saves, O bliss sublime!
Je- sus saves, O mighty pow'r! Je - sus saves, O bliss sublime!

Jesus saves me hour by hour, Je- sus saves me all the time.
Jesus saves me hour by hour, saves me all the time.

From "Hymns of Consecration."

THE UNSEEN COUNTRY.

ADA BLENKHORN.   H. H. McGRANAHAN.

1. Whom shall I meet in the unseen country, Whom shall I meet in that land so fair?
2. What shall I hear in the unseen country, What shall I hear in that land so fair?
3. What shall I see in the unseen country, What shall I see in that land so fair?
4. What shall I do in the unseen country, What shall I do in that land so fair?

Friends who have entered the upper glory, Leaving behind all their grief and care:
Voices of angels the Lamb ador-ing Fall without ceasing upon the air:
Wonderful thrones in that holy cit-y, Visions of glo-ry beyond compare!
Praise without ceasing my precious Saviour, Who for my soul doth a place prepare:

Robed in pure garments of heav'nly brightness, Crowns of e-ter-nal life they wear;
Songs of the ransomed in praise to Jesus, In the glad music I, too, shall share;
Tree of Life for the nations' healing, Life's pure river that floweth there;
This be my joy thro' e-ter-nal a-ges, All of his good-ness to declare;

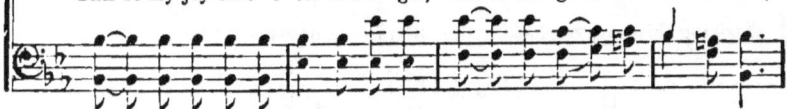

These I shall meet in the unseen country, These I shall meet in that land so fair.
This I shall hear in the unseen country, This I shall hear in that land so fair.
This I shall see in the unseen country, This I shall see in that land so fair.
This I shall do in the unseen country, This I shall do in that land so fair.

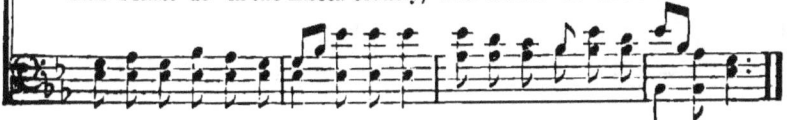

No. 64. LOOKING THIS WAY.

J. W. V.   J. W. VanDeVenter.

DUET.

1. O-ver the riv - er fa-ces I   see, Fair as the morning, looking for me;
2. Father and mother, safe in the vale, Watch for the boatman, wait for the sail,
3. Brother and sister, gone to that clime, Wait for the others, coming sometime;
4. Sweet little darling, light of the home, Looking for someone, beckoning come;
5. Jesus the Saviour, bright morning star, Looking for lost ones, straying afar;

Free from their sorrow, grief and despair, Waiting and watching, patiently there.
Bearing the loved ones o-ver the tide In- to the harbor, near to their side.
Safe with the angels, whiter than snow, Watching for dear ones waiting below.
Bright as a sunbeam, pure as the dew, Anxiously looking, mother, for you.
Hear the glad message; why will you roam? Jesus is calling, "Sinner, come home."

CHORUS.

Looking this way, yes, looking this way; Loved ones are waiting, looking this way;

Fair as the morning, bright as the day, Dear ones in glory looking this way.

No. 65. CALVARY.

"The place which is called Calvary, there they crucified Him."—Luke 23 : 33.

W. M'K. DARWOOD. JNO. R. SWENEY.

Moderato.

1. On Calv'ry's brow............ my Sav-iour died,............'Twas there my
2. 'Mid rending rocks............and dark'ning skies,............ My Sav-iour
3. O Je-sus, Lord,........... how can it be...............That thou shouldst

Lord......... was cru-ci-fied ;.........'Twas on the cross......... He bled for
bows......... His head and dies ;.........The opening vail........... reveals the
give......... Thy life for me, ... To bear the cross......... and ag-o-

me,............... And purchased there............. my par-don free.
way............... To heav-en's joys............. and end-less day.
ny................... In that dread hour.............. on Cal-va-ry?

CHORUS.

O Cal-va-ry! dark Cal-va-ry! Where Je-sus shed His blood for me, for me;

rit. *p*

O Cal-va-ry! blest Cal-va-ry! 'Twas there my Saviour died for me.

SOME SWEET DAY.

Arthur W. French.   D. B. Towner.

Moderato.

1. We shall reach the riv - er side   Some sweet day, some sweet day;
2. We shall pass in - side the gate   Some sweet day, some sweet day;
3. We shall meet our loved and own   Some sweet day, some sweet day;

We shall cross the storm - y tide   Some sweet day, some sweet day;
Peace and plen - ty for us wait   Some sweet day, some sweet day;
Gath'ring round the great white throne   Some sweet day, some sweet day

We shall press the sands of gold,   While be - fore our eyes un - fold
We shall hear the wondrous strain,   Glo - ry to the Lamb that's slain,
By the tree of life so fair,   Joy and rap - ture ev - 'ry- where,

Heav- en's splen- dors, yet un - told,   Some sweet day, some sweet day.
Christ was dead, but lives a - gain,   Some sweet day, some sweet day.
O the bliss of o - ver there!   Some sweet day, some sweet day.

No. 67.　　　　OH, IT IS WONDERFUL.

E. C. GREEN. Rewritten.　　　　　　　Rev. ELISHA A. HOFFMAN.

1. Can it be that Jesus bought me, And on the hallowed cross atoned for me,
2. Praise His name, He sought and found me, Saved me from wandering and brought me near;
3. It was months He had been waiting, Waiting the dawning of the precious hour;
4. From that hour He has been seeking, How He may fill me with His precious love;

Loved me, chose me ere I knew Him? Oh, what a precious, precious Friend is He?
Free - ly now His grace bestowing, Jesus is growing unto me more dear.
When I should at last be yielding, Yielding to Jesus ev'ry ransomed pow'r.
How He may thro' grace transform me, Meet for the fellowship of saints above.

CHORUS.

Oh, it is won-der-ful, ve - ry, ve - ry won-der-ful,

1.
All His grace so rich and free!
[*Omit.* . . . .]

2.
All His love and grace to me!

5 As I think of all, I marvel
　Why in such patience He my good
　　has sought,
　And bestowed His grace upon me,
　And in my spirit such a change
　　has wrought.

6 So I cry, with love o'erflowing:
　"Unto the Savior be eternal
　　praise,"
　Who redeemed me, soul and body.
　Filling with gladness all my
　　earthly days.

No. 68.   'TIS A GREAT SALVATION.

C. H. M.   (Hebrew 2: 3.)   MRS. C. H. MORRIS.

1. How hopeless was the sinner's lot, How sad his lost con-di-tion,
2. Should justice reign, we naught but death And endless hell could mer-it;
3. Not on-ly from the guilt of sin, But from its power he frees us;
4. He o-pens wide the prison doors, And breaks the chains that bind us·
5. His blood a-lone will cleanse from sin, And save from condemna-tion·

Un-til the news came down to earth, For sin there is re-mis-sion.
But bleed-ing Mer-cy speaks, and we E-ter-nal life in-her-it.
'Tis wondrous grace when we be-come New creatures in Christ Je-sus.
And bids us on-ward press, and leave The world and sin behind us.
Then "how shall we es-cape, if we Neglect so great sal-va-tion?"

CHORUS.

'Tis a great sal-va-tion that Je-sus brings, 'Tis a great sal-vation that

Jesus brings; To great sinners this great Saviour A great salvation brings.
To all great sinners this loving Saviour,

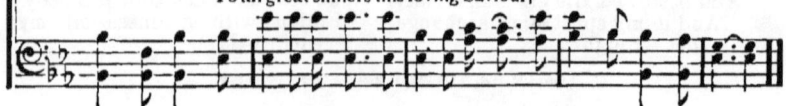

WONDERFUL FULLNESS OF JOY.

J. B. M.   J. B. MACKAY.

1. There is joy in the ser-vice of Je-sus the Lord, No pleasure of
2. One brief day in his ser-vice is bet-ter, by far, Than years of de-
3. Oh! this joy like a deep, crys-tal stream floweth on, Refresh-ing our
4. There is nothing shall tempt us from Je-sus a-way, His love all with-

earth can be-stow; He giv-eth to all who are faithful to him,
vo-tion to sin; The joy of the Lord is e-ter-nal and sure,
souls here be-low; It's source is the won-der-ful fountain of life,
in us con-trols; We know if to him we are faith-ful and true,

D. S.—ser-vice of love for the Sav-iour a-bove

Fine. Chorus.

A joy that the world can-not know.   Joy,   won-der-ful
And rich-ly a-bid-eth with-in.
Whose wa-ters for-ev-er shall flow.
His joy will a-bound in our souls.   Wonderful, wonder-ful

With joy makes our hearts o-ver-flow.

D.S.

full-ness of joy, Joy that the world can-not know; The

No. 70. COUNTLESS MERCIES.

"According to the multitude of his mercies."—Lam. 3: 32.

FLORA KIRKLAND.   CHAS. H. GABRIEL.

1. Are you heavy-laden and with sorrow tried? Stop and look to Jesus, Helper,
2. Think of hidden dangers he hath bro't you thro'; Think of all the burdens he hath
3. Does your pathway darken 'neath a cloud of fear? Count your many mercies; dry each
4. As he looks from heaven now on you and me, Don't you know he chooseth what each

Friend and Guide; Think of all his mercies; such a boundless store!
borne for you; Count his words of comfort in your deep - est need;
bit - ter tear. E- ven 'mid the shadows trust him with - out fear;
day shall be? Trust his lov - ing wis- dom, though the hot tears start,

CHORUS.

Tears will change to praises as you count them o'er. ⎫ Count - less mercies!
Count the times when Jesus proved a Friend indeed. ⎪
"Home will be the sweeter for the dark down here." ⎬
Give to him the incense of a grate - ful heart. ⎭ Countless mercies! such a

such a boundless store! Countless mercies! pressed and running o'er! Countless
boundless store! Countless mercies! pressed and run - ning o'er! Countless mercies!

mercies! try to count them o'er Till you gaze in wonder at your boundless store.
try to count them o'er

No. 71.   WHEN JESUS COMES IN HIS GLORY.

E. E. Hewitt.
Moderato.

Wm. J. Kirkpatrick.

1. Time hur-ries on-ward with fast-fly-ing feet, Shall we be read-y the
2. Bliss beyond tell-ing to those who shall rise, Meet-ing the King and his
3. Toil on, be-liev-er, there's blessed re-ward, Cheer up, sad heart-ed, there's
4. Car-ing for those who still wander a-way, O let us gath-er them

Mas-ter to meet When he de-scends from the bright, gold-en street?
host in the skies, See-ing his beau-ty with love's ravished eyes,
joy in the Lord, Some day you'll sing to re-demp-tion's full chord,
in while we may, O to be watch-ing when dawns the great day,

CHORUS.

When Je-sus comes in his glo-ry. When Je-sus comes in his glo-ry,

When Je-sus comes in his glo-ry, Will we haste to meet him,

rit.

And re-joice to greet him, When Je-sus comes in his glo-ry?

HEART YEARNINGS.

R. O. Smith.

W. S. Weeden.

1. My soul is pant-ing to be free From all its car-nal load,
2. I walk when I should swift-ly run, And run when I should fly;
3. O quick-ly break each curs-ed chain That keeps my soul a-way
4. Help me to scale the ho-ly height Of pure and per-fect love,

And fath-om the im-men-si-ty Of all the love of God!
O Christ, my Lord, thou mighty One, Come, help me, lest I die!
From all the heights of ec-sta-sy It yearns to find in thee.
And dwelling ev-er in thy light I'll reign with thee a-bove.

CHORUS.

Lord, fill my soul! O fill my soul With power from on high!

I hun-ger af-ter righteousness; Lord, fill me, or I die.

No. 73.

HEART ECHOES.

Miss Carrie Butcher.

Charlie D. Tillman.

1. I'm the child of a King, And with rapture I sing, Not a care can my
(Gal. 4: 5-7.)   (Isa. 12: 5.)
2. True, there once was a time When no answering chime Sweetly thrilled to the

comfort destroy; O I'm glad all the day, And I shout on my way,
(1 Peter 5: 7.)   (Ps. 16: 8, 9.)   (Is. 12: 6.)
dis- cord without, But since Je - sus came in, Now he qui - ets the din,
(Rev. 3: 20.)   (John 16: 33.)

CHORUS.

While my heart's brimming over with joy. }
(Ps. 16: 11.)   } When he reigns in the heart, Ev'ry
He alone brought these wonders about.

grief must depart; Where he dwells, not a shadow is found; If for him you make

room, He will banish the gloom, Spreading gladness and sunshine around.

3 If we let him abide, (Ps. 32: 8.)
O how smoothly we glide; (Isa. 32: 17.)
   Now, safe anchored, no tempest can more,
What though riches take wing,
He extracts every sting,
   And his banner around us is love. (Cant. 2: 4.)

4 Thus we speed on our ways,
Clad in garments of praise. (Isa. 61: 3.)
   With our Lord's Gospel sandals we're shod. (Eph. 6: 15.)
In his might, O how strong, (Prov. 18: 10.)
We can never go wrong,
   While abiding and hiding in God. (John 15: 10.)

EVERYTHING FOR JESUS.

FLORA KIRKLAND.   W. I. SOUTHERTON.

1. Ev'rything for Je-sus! this my joyous song; All I am and all I
2. Ev'rything for Je-sus! Lord, I pray to-day, Cleanse me for thy service,
3. An-ything thou sendest, be it joy or pain; Anything thou choosest,

have to him be-long; All my heav-y bur-dens at his feet I place;
purge my faults a-way; Let me hold earth's treasures with a loosened clasp,
be it loss or gain, Help me whisper al-ways, "Not my will, but thine;"

D.S.—Praying thee to help me live each day and hour,

Fine. CHORUS.

Liv-ing in the sunshine of his blessed face.
Help me yield my weakness to thy mighty grasp. } Ev'rything! Ev'rything!
Fit me, Lord, for service by thy touch divine.

Shining out my wit-ness to thy saving pow'r.

D.S.

still my gift is small; Je-sus, my Re-deemer, at thy feet I fall;

No. 75.

FACE TO FACE.

Mrs. FRANK A. BRECK.

GRANT COLFAX TULLAR.

Moderato.

1. Face to face with Christ my Sav-iour, Face to face—what will it be?
2. On - ly faint-ly now, I see him, With the darkling veil be-tween,
3. What re-joic-ing in his pres-ence, When are banished grief and pain;
4. Face to face! O! blissful mo-ment! Face to face—to see and know;

When with rapture I be - hold him, Je-sus Christ who died for me.
But a bless-ed day is com - ing, When his glo - ry shall be seen.
When the crooked ways are straightened,And the dark things shall be plain.
Face to face with my Re- deem - er, Je-sus Christ who loves me so.

CHORUS.

Face to face shall I be - hold him, Far beyond the starry sky;

Face to face in all his glo - ry, I shall see him by and by!

No. 76.   SUNLIGHT.

J. W. Van De Venter.   W. S. Weeden.

1. I wan-dered in the shades of night, Till Je - sus came to me,
2. Though clouds may gather in the sky, And bil-lows round me roll,
3. While walk - ing in the light of God, I, sweet com-mun - ion find ;
4. I cross the wide ex-tend - ed fields, I jour - ney o'er the plains,
5. Soon I shall see him as he is, The Light that came to me ;

And with the sun - light of his love Bid all my dark-ness flee.
How - ev - er dark the world may be I've sun-light in my soul.
I press with ho - ly vig - or on And leave the world be - hind.
And in the sun - light of his love I reap the gold - en grain.
Be - hold the brightness of his face, Throughout e - ter - ni - ty.

CHORUS.

Sun-light, sun-light, in my soul to - day, Sun-light, sun-light
to - day, yes,

all a - long the way, Since the Sav - iour found me,
nar - row way,

took a - way my sin, I have had the sunlight of his love with-in.
load of sin,

No. 77. HAVE YOU FOUND THE SAVIOUR PRECIOUS?

IDA L. REED. J. LINCOLN HALL.

1. Have you found the Sav-iour pre- cious? More than all on earth be - side,
2. Have you found the Sav-iour pre- cious? Who for you passed thro' the grave,
3. Have you found the Sav-iour pre- cious? Do you know the peace and rest,
4. Have you found the Sav-iour pre- cious? Seek Him then with-out de - lay,

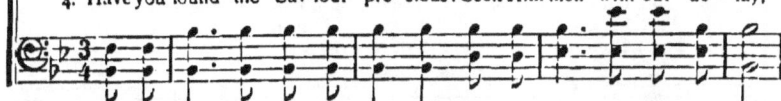

He who gave His life to save you, Who for your transgress-ions died?
Broke the bonds of death a - sun- der, Have you "proved His pow'r to save?"
That doth fill each soul that trusts Him ; Who in His deep love is blest?
Taste the sweet- ness of His par - don, He will take our sins a - way.

CHORUS.

Have you found the Sav - iour pre - cious? Can you
Have you found, found this friend? Can you

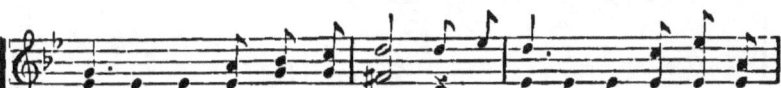

slight such love as this, Sure- ly there can be no
slight, you slight, such love as this, Sure- ly there can be no

great - er, Would you give your life for His?
great - er love, Would you, give your life for His? (for His?)

No. 78. OUT INTO THE LIGHT.

HELEN B. MONTGOMERY.

W. S. WEEDEN.

1. Sing, hap-py song in my heart, to-night, Sing, yes, sing!
2. Low on thy knees, oh, my soul be thou, Pray, yes, pray!
3. Up from thy knees, with an ear-nest will; Work, yes, work
4. Pa-tience, my soul, tho' the way be long · Wait, yes, wait!
5. Trust, then my soul, thro' the dark-est night, Trust, then trust!

I have been help'd by the Lord of might In leading a broth-er out
Ask Him to teach thee and show thee how The heart of an-other to
God for thy la-bor shall give thee skill, And all His good pleas-ure
God and thy pray-ers are still more strong, Than all the dread bon-dage
God knows thy fears and thy hopes so bright, He leads thy lov'd ones out

CHORUS.

in - to the light, Sing, yes, sing!
reach just now, Pray, yes, pray:
in thee fulfill, Work, yes, work!
of sin and wrong, Wait, yes, wait:
in - to the light, Trust, then trust!

O joy that li-eth for words too deep,

Joy of the Shepherd who findeth His sheep: Then drink, of that joy, oh, my

Rit.

soul, to-night!   Lead-ing an-oth-er out in-to the light.

No. 79. SAVED THROUGH JESUS' BLOOD.

J. W. V.   J. W. VanDeVenter.

1. Sometime we'll stand before the judgment bar, The quick, the risen dead;
2. I'll then receive a bright and star-ry crown, As on - ly God can give;
3. Then we shall meet to never part a - gain; Our toil will then be o'er;

The Lord will then make known the record there; Our names will all be read.
And when I've been with him ten thousand years, I'll have no less to live.
We'll lay our burdens down at Je - sus' feet, And rest for - ev - er more.

CHORUS.

I'll be present when the roll is called, Pure and spotless thro' the crimson flood;

I will an-swer when they call my name; Saved thro' Je - sus blood.

No. 80. MY SAVIOUR.

A. A. Payn.

C. Austin Miles.

1. He will hear me when I call, He will help me when I fall, My Saviour, my
2. I will la-bor, I will pray, I will trust him ev'ry day, My Saviour, my
3. When I'm weary and distressed, I will go to him for rest, My Saviour, my
4. May I nev-er, never stray From thy precious side away, My Saviour, my

Saviour; He will give me strength to bear Ev'ry grief that may appear; My
Sav - iour; I will look to him in faith, I will trust him un-til death; My
Sav - iour; To his loving arms I'll fly, Ev-'ry need he will supply, My
Sav - iour; Naught of e- vil will I fear, While I have my Saviour near; My

CHORUS.

all in all is he. Yes, a sat - is - fy- ing portion is my Saviour, My

Saviour, my Saviour; My rock, my stay, by night and day My all in all is he.

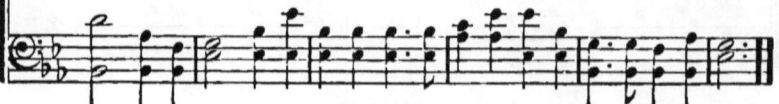

No. 81.   WONDERFUL PEACE.

Rev. W. D. Cornell. Alt.   Rev. W. G. Cooper.

1. Far - a - way in the depths of my spir - it to - night, Rolls a
2. What a treas - ure I have in this won - der - ful peace, Bur - ied
3. I am rest - ing to - night in this won - der - ful peace, Rest-ing
4. And me thinks when I rise to that Cit - y of peace, Where the
5. Ah! soul, are you here with - out com - fort or rest, Marching

mel - o - dy sweet-er than psalm; In ce - les - tial like strains it un -
deep in the heart of my soul; So se - cure that no pow - er can
sweet - ly in Je - sus' con - trol; For I'm kept from all dan - ger by
Au - thor of peace I shall see, That one strain of the song which the
down the rough pathway of time! Make Je - sus your friend ere the

ceas - ing - ly falls O'er my soul like an in - fi - nite calm.
mine it a - way, While the years of e - ter - ni - ty roll.
night and by day, And his glo - ry is flood - ing my soul.
ransomed will sing, In that heav - en - ly king-dom will be,
shadows grow dark; O ac - cept of this peace so sub - lime.

CHORUS.

Peace! Peace! Wonderful peace, Coming down from the Father a - bove; Sweep

o - ver my spirit for - ev - er, I pray, In fathomless billows of love.

No. 82.   CALVARY.

Rev. R. Carradine, D. D.   Jno. R. Bryan.

1. There's a hill lone and gray, In a land far a-way, In a country be-
2. Behold! faint on the road, 'Neath a world's heavy load, Comes a thorn-crowned
3. Hark! I hear the dull blow Of the hammer swung low; They are nailing my
4. How they mock him in death To his last lab'ring breath, While his friends sadly

yond the blue sea, Where beneath that fair sky Went a man forth to die,
man on the way, With a cross he is bow'd, But still on thro' the crowd
Lord to the tree! And the cross they upraise, While the mul-ti-tude gaze
weep o'er the way! But tho' lone-ly and faint, Still no word of complaint

D.S.—For 'twas there on its side   Je-sus suf-fered and died,

FINE. REFRAIN.

For the world, and for you, and for   me.
He's as-cend-ing that hill lone and gray. }
On the blest Lamb of dark Cal-va-ry.   }   O, it bows down my heart,
Fell from him on the hill lone and gray.

To re-deem a poor sin-ner like me.

D.S.

And the tear-drops will start, When in mem'ry that gray hill   I   see;

5 Then darkness came down,
   And the rocks rent around,
      And a cry pierced the grief-laden air!
   'Twas the voice of our King,
   Who received death's dark sting,
      All to save us from endless despair!

6 Let the sun hide its face,
   Let the earth reel apace,
      Over men who their Saviour have [slain!
   But, behold! from the sod,
   Comes the blest Lamb of God,
      Who was slain, but is risen again!

No. 83.　　　　WILL THERE BE ANY STARS?

E. E. Hewitt.　　　　　　　　　　　　　　　　Jno. R. Sweney.

1. I am thinking to-day of that beau ti - ful land I shall reach when the
2. In the strength of the Lord let me la - bor and pray, Let me watch as a
3. Oh, what joy will it be when his face I be-hold Living gems at his

sun goeth down; When thro' wonderful grace by my Saviour I stand, Will there
winner of souls; That bright stars may be mine in the glorious day, When his
feet to lay down; It would sweeten my bliss in the city of gold, Should there

CHORUS.

be an-y stars in my crown?
praise like the sea billow rolls. } Will there be any stars, any stars in my crown,
be an-y stars in my crown.

When at evening the sun go-eth down?...... When I wake with the blest
go-eth down?

In the man-sions of rest, Will there be an - y stars in my crown?.....
an - y stars in my crown?

No. 84. JESUS SWEETLY SAVES.

Mrs. C. H. M. 4th verse by H. L. G. Mrs. C. H. MORRIS.

1. I had heard the gos-pel call, of-fering par-don free for all, And I
2. Now the load of sin is gone, and by faith I trav-el on, And I
3. From the mire and from the clay, Je-sus took my feet a-way And He
4. When I reach the gold-en street, and the loved ones gladly meet, The re-

hearkened to the bless-ed in-vi-ta-tion; Laid my sins at Je-sus'
rest no long-er un-der con-dem-na-tion; For the blood has been ap-
placed them on the Rock, the sure Founda-tion; Whether now I live or
deemed which came out of great tribu-la-tion, Having washed their garments

feet, tast-ed there re-demp-tion sweet, And He saved me with an
plied, and my soul is sat-is-fied With this full, and free, this
die, this shall be my con-stant cry Je-sus saves me with an
white, prais-ing God both day and night For this full, and free, this

CHORUS.

ut-ter-most sal-va-tion. Je-sus saves, sweetly saves, Je-sus
Je-sus saves, sweetly saves,

saves me with an ut-ter-most sal-va-tion; Tho' I can-not tell you how.

JESUS SWEETLY SAVES.—Concluded.

Je-sus sweetly saves me now, With a full, and free, an uttermost salva-tion.

No. 85.   ## WHOSOEVER WILL MAY COME.

FANNY J. CROSBY.   STEPHEN C. FOSTER.

1. O   ye thirst-y ones that lan-guish, On life's drifting sand,
2. From the riv-er gent-ly flow-ing Drink a   full sup-ply;
3. O   the bliss of life e-ter-nal! You may al-so share;
4. Lo, the summer days are end-ing, They will soon be o'er;

Fine.

'Tis the Saviour bending o'er you, Reaching out his toil worn hand.
Free to all its blessed wa-ters, Wherefore will ye faint and die?
Come to Je-sus, and be-liev-ing, En-ter thro' the gate of prayer.
While the Spir-it still is plead-ing, Grieve your dearest Friend no more.

D.S.—To the lov-ing arms of mer-cy Who-so-ev-er will may come.

CHORUS.   *D.S.*

Why   will   ye   wan-der,   Far   a-way   from   home?

IS YOUR LAMP BURNING?

Mrs. Jos. F. Knapp.

1. Say, is your lamp burning? O Christian, I pray you look quickly and
2. Re-member how ma - ny a - round you Will fol- low wherev- er you
3. There's many a lamp that is lighted, We see them from near and from
4. But if they were trimmed night and morning They'd never burn down nor go

see, For if it were burning, then surely Some beams would fall brightly on
go; The tho't that they walk'd in your shadow Would make your lamp brighter I
far, But few in their lustre and beau - ty Shine stead- i - ly on like a
out, Tho' from the four quarters of heav- en The winds were all blowing a-

CHORUS.

me, Some beams would fall brightly on me.
know, Would make your lamp brighter I know.
star, Shine steadi- ly on like a ' star.
bout, The winds were all blowing about.

} Lift your lamp higher, Lift your lamp

higher, higher, still higher; Then lift your lamp higher, O Christian,

Lest some should make fatal delay.

5 If once all the lamps that are lighted
Should steadily blaze in a line,
Wide over the land and the ocean
||: A girdle of glory would shine. :||

6 How all the dark places would brighten !
The mists would roll up and away !
The earth would laugh out in her gladness
||: To hail the millennial day ! :||

No. 87. TRUTH TRIUMPHANT.

"God shall send forth his mercy and his truth."—Ps. 57 : 3.

GRACE REED OLIVER.

1. My soul has seen a vis-ion of the con-quest of the world, When
2. No more shall strife and ha-tred bring dis-hon-or to our God, For
3. The des-ert place shall blos-som; and the wil-derness re-joice, The
4. My soul has heard the tri-umph song that ris-es from the plain, It

Sa-tan and his fore-es from their bat-tle-ments are hurled, And
right-eous-ness, whose work is peace, shall spread her wings a-broad, And
lame shall leap, the blind shall see, the dumb lift up their voice; The
ech-oes and re-ech-oes from the mountain-tops a-gain; In

o'er the land the Bi-ble, like a sig-nal flag unfurled, Speaks
they who win the con-quest are the bear-ers of the word, In
floods shall clap their hands, the earth shall make a joy-ful noise, In
grand and might-y cho-rus let us swell the loft-y strain Of

CHORUS.

loy-al-ty to Christ. We shall see the truth so glorious Over all the earth vic-

to-rious, For the standard lift ed o-ver us Is loy-al-ty to Christ.

No. 88. WHEN OUR SHIPS COME SAILING HOME.

Rev. Johnson Oatman, Jr.

Jno. R. Sweney.

1. When our ships have crossed the o - cean, and been all a - round the world,
2. But if there is such re - joic - ing to see ves - sels here get home,
3. Oh, methinks I hear the an - gels shout, "here comes an earthly bark,
4. So with Je - sus as our Cap-tain we ex - pect to gain that shore,

When they safe - ly gain the ha - ven, and their sails a - gain are furled;
When we know that in a lit - tle while these ships a - gain will roam;
She has found her way to heav - en, tho' the way was rough and dark;
We ex - pect to cast our an-chor there, and stay for - ev - er more;

We re - joice to see them en - ter, and to know the an-chor's cast,
Oh, what must it be in heav - en when a soul comes sail - ing in,
But she had a star to guide her, called the bright and morn-ing star,
And we know the an - gels will be there to greet us when we come,

Rais- ing joy - ful shouts of wel-come, for our ships are home at last.
To go out no more for - ev - er sail-ing on the sea of sin?
It has guid-ed mill-ions o - ver from that dis - tant land a - far."
They will join in songs of rap-ture, "welcome home, oh, wel-come home."

CHORUS.

Oh, what sing-ing, oh, what shouting, when our ships come sail - ing home;

WHEN OUR SHIPS COME SAILING HOME.—Concluded.

They have stood the mighty tempests, they have crossed the o - cean's foam ;

They have passed o'er stormy bil-lows, but they now have gained the shore,

The au-chor's cast, they're home at last, the voyage is safe - ly o'er.

No. 89.   **GOD CALLING YET.**

Tr. Jane Borthwick.   John E. Gould.

1. God call-ing yet! shall I not hear? Earth's pleasures shall I still hold dear?
2. God call-ing yet! shall I not rise? Can I His lov-ing voice de-spise,
3. God call-ing yet! and shall He knock, And I my heart the clos - er lock?
4. God call-ing yet! I can-not stay; My heart I yield without de - lay:

Shall life's swift passing years all fly, And still my soul in slumbers lie?
And basely His kind care re - pay? He calls me still; can I de - lay?
He still is wait-ing to re - ceive, And shall I dare His Spir-it grieve?
Vain world, farewell! from thee I part; The voice of God hath reached my heart.

No. 90.   PLEADING WITH THEE.

ELISHA A. HOFFMAN.   R. M. McINTOSH.

1. There is a voice of the ten-der-est love Plead-ing with thee,
2. Long he has stood at the door of thy heart, Wait-ing on thee,
3. Do you not hear him as gen-tly he pleads, Call-ing to thee,
4. O how he yearns o'er thy sin-burdened-heart, Whisp'ring to thee,

plead-ing with thee; It is the voice of the Lord from a-bove,
wait-ing on thee; Read-y his grace and his peace to im-part,
call-ing to thee? See with what fer-vor the Lord in-ter-cedes,
whisp'ring to thee; Earn-est-ly longs his sweet love to im-part,

CHORUS.

Say-ing, "O come un-to me." "Come un-to me,...........
"Come un-to me,

come un-to me,"................ Je-sus is ten-der-ly
come un-to me,"

call-ing to thee. "Come un-to me,........... come un-to
"Come un-to me,

By per. Barbee & Smith, Agents, Publishing House M. E. Church, South.

PLEADING WITH THEE.—Concluded.

me,"..............   Je - sus is ten - der - ly call - ing to thee.
come un - to me,"

No. 91.   ## WHILE JESUS WHISPERS.

"Come unto me."—Matt. 11 : 28.

WILL. E. WITTER.   H. R. PALMER.

1. While Je - sus whis-pers to you, Come, sin-ner, come! While we are
2. Are you too heav - y la- den? Come, sin-ner, come! Je - sus will
3. Oh, hear his ten-der pleading, Come, sin-ner, come! Come and re-

pray-ing for you, Come, sin-ner, come! Now is the time to own Him,
bear your burden, Come, sin-ner, come! Je - sus will not de-ceive you,
ceive his bless-ing, Come, sin-ner, come! While Je - sus whispers to you,

Come, sin-ner, come! Now is the time to know him, Come, sinner, come!
Come, sin-ner, come! Je - sus can now redeem you, Come, sinner, come!
Come, sin-ner, come! While we are pray-ing for you, Come, sinner, come!

No. 92.   NEVER ALONE.

E. E. Hewitt.

J. C. H. and V. A. White.

1. "Fear not, I am with thee;" Bless-ed gold-en ray, Like a star of
2. Ros - es fade a-round me, Lil - ies bloom and die, Earth-ly sunbeams
3. Steps un-seen be- fore me, Hid-den dangers near; Near - er still my

glo - ry, Light- ing up my way! Throu'h the clouds of mid- night,
van - ish— Ra - diant still the sky! Je - sus, Rose of Shar - on,
Sav - iour, Whisp'ring, "be of cheer," Joy like birds of spring-time,

This bright promise shone, "I will nev-er leave thee, Nev - er will
Bloom-ing for His own. Je - sus, Heaven's sun- shine, Nev - er will
To my heart have flown, Sing- ing all so sweet- ly, "He will not

CHORUS.

leave thee a - lone." }
leave me a - lone. } No,   nev - er a - lone,..............
leave me a - lone." } Nev - er a - lone,   nev - er a- lone,

No, nev - er a - lone, He prom- ised nev - er to leave me,

Nev-er to leave me a - lone.   Nev-er to leave me a - lone.

No. 93.   ON THE VICTORY SIDE.

JAMES L. BLACK.   JNO. R. SWENEY.

1. Our souls cry out, hal- le - lu - jah! And our faith en - rap-tured sings,
2. Our souls cry out, hal- le - lu - jah! For the Lord him-self comes near,
3. Our souls cry out, hal- le - lu - jah! For the tempter flies a - pace,
4. Our souls cry out, hal- le - lu - jah! And our hearts beat high with praise,

While we throw to the breeze the standard Of the might-y King of kings.
And the shout of a roy - al ar - my On the bat - tle-field we hear.
And the chains he has forged are breaking, Thro' the pow'r of redeeming grace.
Un - to him, in whose name we'll conquer, And our song of triumph raise.

CHORUS.

On the vic-t'ry side, on the vic- t'ry side, In the ranks of the Lord are we;

On the vic- t'ry side we will bold- ly stand, Till the glo- ry land we see.

WONDERFUL SAVIOUR.

FANNY J. CROSBY.   MRS. JOS. F. KNAPP.

1. Won - der - ful Sav - iour, bless - ed Redeem - er, Ev - er in glo - ry,
2. Sing of his greatness, in - fi - nite greatness, Sing of his goodness
3. He is our ref - uge, he is our safe-guard, Peace to the youthful

dwelling a - bove; Yet in his mer - cy tender- ly smiling, Over the
day aft - er day; Guarding from e - vil, shielding from danger, Leading us
kindly he brings; Sweet is the promise he will protect us, He will de-

CHORUS.

children bending in love. }
onward, cheering the way. } We will adore him, gather and praise him,
fend us under his wings. }

Voic - es in con - cert joy - ful - ly blend; His be the kingdom,

power and glo - ry, Now and for-ev - er, world without end; His be the kingdom, power and glo - ry, Now and for-ev - er, world without end.

No. 95.   **THE DAY-BREAK SONG.**

* * * "Until the day dawn, and the daystar arise in your hearts."—2 Peter 1: 19.

Rev. Johnson Oatman, Jr.   Geo. F. Rosche.

1. Lift your eyes, the day is break - ing, Tho' the night was dark and long;
2. Sinner, look to Calv'ry's mountain; See, the day begins to dawn,
3. The Mil- len- ni- um is near - ing, And the time will not be long;
4. When life's twilight hour is end - ed, Lean upon God's arm so strong,

Fine.

Sinners from their sleep are wak - ing, Come and join the day-break song.
Lighting up the healing fount - ain, Come and join the day-break song.
Hark ! the sons of God are cheer - ing, Come and join the day-break song.
And with those who have as- cend - ed, Come and join the day-break song.

D.S.—Tell the world redemption's sto - ry, Come and join the day-break song.

Chorus.   *D.S.*

See, the earth is full of glo - ry, Right shall triumph o - ver wrong;

I WILL BEAR THE CROSS.

C. A. M.

C. Austin Miles.

DUET. ALTO AND TENOR.

1. Je - sus, my Saviour, when I stand and view thy cross, Lov - ing thee
2. Je - sus, my Saviour, thou didst bear the cros for me   In tears and
3. Hear me, O Je-sus, as be-fore thy throne I kneel; While I am

on - ly, all of self is dross; Shall I, O guiltless Saviour, in dis-
anguish that I might be free, And I, in sinful blindness, Have re-
waiting, thy dear self re - veal; And I, the answer waiting, Looking

dain thy suff'rings see? Can I forget, O Jesus, thou didst bear the cross for me?
fused thee as my Guide, Nor felt thro' years of wand'ring,'twas for me that thou hast died.
up thro' toil and pain To thee, my coming Saviour, who hath died, but lives again.

CHORUS.

I...... will bear the cross for Jesus, I...... will bear the cross for Jesus,
I will bear the cross,   I will bear the cross,

I...... will bear the cross for Je - sus; He bore the cross for me.
I will bear the cross,   for me.

HAPPY DAY.

A. W. S.

A. W. SPOONER

1. Yes, the time is drawing nearer, happy day, When the clouds that hide our
2. Yes, the time is drawing nearer, blessed dawn, When our arms shall clasp the
3. Yes, the time is drawing nearer, O how blest, When our weary hearts shall
4. Yes, the time is drawing nearer; one by one To e-ter-ni-ty the

path shall roll a - way; We shall know as we are known, When we
loved ones from us torn; In that home beyond the tomb Partings
gath - er home to rest; We shall walk the gold - en street, And our
moments swift- ly run; Soon the trum - pet will resound, All the

stand be - fore the throne, Stand complete in Christ a- lone; Happy day.
nev - er, nev - er come, And we ne'er shall walk a- lone; Happy day.
loved ones there shall meet, Life with Je- sus will be sweet; Happy day.
dead shall hear the sound, Loving hearts with joy shall bound; Happy day.

CHORUS.

Happy day; Sins all washed away; We'll be home at last, home to stay;
glad day;

At the Saviour's feet, It will be so sweet; O what joy the King to greet; Happy day.

No. 98. THE CHILD OF A KING.

HATTIE E. BUELL.   Rev. JOHN B. SUMNER, arr.

1. My Fa - ther is rich in hous - es and lands, He hold-eth the
2. My Fa-ther's own Son, the Sav - iour of men, Once wander'd o'er
3. I once was an out - cast stran - ger on earth, A sin - ner by
4. A tent or a cot - tage, why should I care? They're building a

wealth of the world in his hands! Of ru - bies and dia-monds of
earth as the poor - est of men, But now he is reign - ing for-
choice, an al - ien by birth! But I've been a - dopt - ed, my
pal - ace for me o - ver there! Tho' ex - il - ed from home, yet,

sil - ver and gold His cof - fers are full,—he has rich - es un - told.
ev - er on high, And will give me a home in heaven by and by.
name's written down,—An heir to a man - sion, a robe, and a crown.
still I may sing: All glo - ry to God, I'm the child of a King.

CHORUS.

I'm the child of a King, The child of a King;

ad lib.

With Je - sus my Sav - iour I'm the child of a King.

No. 99. JUST BECAUSE HE LOVED ME SO.

Rev. F. L. Snyder.   Howard E. Smith.

1. O the matchless love of Je - sus, Far ex- ceed- ing aught I know;
2. O that matchless love un-measured, And the heal- ing, cleansing flow,
3. O the matchless love of Je - sus I would e'er to oth - ers show;
4. O the matchless love of Je - sus, I would nev - er let it go;

That he gave his life on Cal - v'ry, Just because he loved me so.
From the pre-cious side of Je - sus, Just because he loved me so.
How my sins he has for-giv - en, Just because he loved me so.
For he promised to be with me, Just because he loved me so.

Chorus.

Just because he loved me so, Just because he loved me so;

Free - ly gave his life a ran - som, Just because he loved me so.

IS IT NOT WONDERFUL?

E. A. H.   Rev. Elisha A. Hoffman.

1. Wondrous it seem - eth to me,   Je - sus so grac - ious should be,
2. Heart of mine nev - er could know   Je - sus such peace could be-stow,
3. Once I was full of all sin,   Now, thro' the blood, I am clean;
4. Long I re - sist - ed his grace,   In my heart gave him no place,
5. He doth my new heart con - trol,   Cleansing and keep - ing me whole,

Mer-cy re-veal-ing, comfort-ing, healing, Blessing a sin - ner like me.
Till the dear Saviour showed me his favor, Cleansed my heart whiter than snow.
Willing to save me, par-don he gave me, And I am hap - py with-in.
But Jesus sought me till he had brought me, Pen - i-tent, seeking his face.
Banishing sadness, with joy and gladness Fill-ing and thrilling my soul.

CHORUS.

{ Is   it not won - der - ful,   is   it not won - der - ful   Je - sus so
{ Yes, it is won - der - ful, strange and so   won - der - ful   (Omit.)

gracious should be?........   :|| That he should save e - ven me!........
loving and gracious should be? :|| That he should par-don and save even me!

No. 101. HE'LL NEVER FORSAKE.

Frank H. Mashaw.   J. Lincoln Hall.

1. "I will fail thee never;" blessed words of cheer, Like a blaze of glo-ry,
2. "I will fail thee never;" tho' the night be long; Soon the morning cometh
3. "I will fail thee never;" brightest flow'rs will fade, But my trust in Jesus
4. "I will fail thee never;" fails the earth and sky, But his bow of promise

shining far and near; Tho' the storm and tempest all around may shake,
with its light and song; Precious words of comfort to my heart I take;
ne'er shall be betrayed; Midnight all around me, soon his light will break,
shineth still on high; Earthly sunbeams vanish, and my heart may quake,

Je-sus, my Saviour, has promised that he will nev-er for-sake.

Chorus.

No, he'll never for-sake,..... No, he'll never for-sake;.... Dangers a-
Never forsake,   Never forsake;

round me may threaten, Jesus will never forsake. :‖ Jesus will never forsake.

No. 102. SPEAK TO MY SOUL.

L. L. P.

Adapted by L. L. PICKETT.

1. Speak to my soul, dear Je - sus, Speak now in tend'rest tone; Whisper in
2. Speak to thy children ev - er, Lead in the ho - ly way; Fill them with
3. Speak now as in the old time Thou didst reveal thy will; Let me know

lov-ing kindness: "Thou art not left a - lone." O-pen my heart to hear thee,
joy and gladness, Teach them to watch and pray. May they in consecra-tion
all my du - ty, Let me thy law ful - fill. Lead me to glo - ri - fy thee,

Quickly to hear thy voice, Fill thou my soul with praises. Let me in thee rejoice.
Yield their whole lives to thee, Hasten thy coming kingdom, Till our dear Lord we see.
Help me to show thy praise, Gladly to do thy bid-ding, Honor thee all my days.

CHORUS.

{ Speak thou in soft - est whis - pers, Whis-pers of love to me;
Speak thou to me each day, Lord, Al-ways in ten-d'rest tone;

1.
"Thou shalt be al-ways conq'ror, Thou shalt be al-ways free."
2.
Let me now hear thy whisper, "Thou art not left (*Omit*.......) a - lone." }

No. 103. JESUS OF NAZARETH PASSETH BY.

Miss Etta Campbell.   Mark 10: 47.   Theo. E. Perkins.

1. What means this eager, anxious throng, Which moves with busy haste along—
2. Who is this Jesus? Why should he The cit - y move so might-i - ly?
3. J sus! 'Tis he who once below Man's pathway trod, 'mid pain and woe;
4. Again he comes! From place to place His ho-ly footprints we can trace.

These wondrous gath'rings day by day? What means this strange commotion pray?
A pass-ing stranger, has he skill To move the mul-ti-tude at will?
And burdened ones, where'er he came, Brought out their sick and deaf and lame.
He pauseth at our threshhold—nay, He en-ters—condescends to stay.

In accents hushed the throng reply: "Je-sus of Naz-areth passeth by,"
Again the stirring notes re-ply: "Je-sus of Naz-areth passeth by,"
The blind rejoiced to hear the cry: "Je-sus of Naz-areth passeth by,"
Shall we not glad-ly raise the cry—"Je-sus of Naz-areth passeth by,"

In accents hushed the throng reply: "Je-sus of Naz-areth passeth by."
Again the stirring notes re-ply: "Je-sus of Naz-areth passeth by."
The blind rejoiced to hear the cry: "Je-sus of Naz-areth passeth by."
Shall we not glad-ly raise the cry—"Je-sus of Naz-areth passeth by."

5 Ho! All ye heavy-laden, come!
  Here's pardon, comfort, rest and home.
  Ye wand'rers from a Father's face,
  Return, accept his proffered grace.
‖: Ye tempted ones, there's refuge nigh:
  "Jesus of Nazareth passeth by." :‖

6 But if you still this call refuse,
  And all his wondrous love abuse,
  Soon will he sadly from you turn,
  Your bitter prayer for pardon spurn.
‖: "Too late! Too late!" will be the cry—
  "Jesus of Nazareth *has passed by*." :‖

No. 104. O BLESSED HOPE.

SOLO, DUET OR QUARTET.

E. E. HEWITT.   WM. J. KIRKPATRICK.

1.   O bless - ed hope so dear, so bright, It cheers the watches of the night;
2.   When dawns that hour of wondrous grace. No veil will hide my Saviour's face;
3.   Sin, pain and death, on that sweet day, Like broken dreams, shall pass away;
4.   Soon, soon shall fade the scenes of time, Im-manuel's advent bells shall chime;

It wakes a song with in the soul, 'Till heav'nly hal - le- lu - jahs roll.
He'll own me ev - er-more as his, And I shall see him as he is.
His spot-less beau- ty I shall wear, His per-fect joy and glo - ry share.
The Bride shall hear the Bridegroom's voice; Look up, my heart, in him rejoice!

CHORUS. 1 John 3: 2.

Be - lov-ed, be- lov - ed, Now are we the sons of God, And it doth not

yet ap-pear what we shall be; But we know that when he shall appear,
we know

We know that when he shall ap- pear, We shall be like him, We shall be
we know

O BLESSED HOPE.—Concluded.

poco ritard.

like him; For we shall see him as he is, We shall see him as he is;

a tempo.

We know that when he shall appear, We know that when he shall appear,
we know   we know

We shall be like him, We shall be like him; For we shall see him as he is.

No. 105.   BY COOL SILOAM'S SHADY RILL.

1. By   cool   Si - lo - am's sha - dy   rill   How sweet the lil - y grows!
2. Lo!   such   a child whose earl-y   feet   The paths of peace have trod,
3. By   cool   Si - lo - am's sha - dy   rill   The lil - y   must de - cay;
4. O   thou who giv - est life   and breath, We ask   thy grace a - lone,

How sweet the breath, be - neath the hill,   Of   Shar - on's dew - y   rose.
Whose sa - cred heart, with influence sweet, Is   up- ward drawn to God.
The   rose that blooms be- neath the hill   Must short-ly fade   a - way.
In   childhood, man- hood, age and death, To   keep us still thine own.

TRUST AND OBEY.

Rev. J. H. Sammis. D. B. Towner.

1. When we walk with the Lord In the light of his word, What a glo-ry he
2. Not a shad-ow can rise, Not a cloud in the skies, But his smile quickly
3. Not a bur-den we bear, Not a sor-row we share, But our toil he doth

sheds on our way! While we do his good will, He a-bides with us
drives it a-way; Not a doubt nor a fear, Not a sigh nor a
rich-ly re-pay; Not a grief nor a loss, Not a frown nor a

CHORUS.

still, And with all who will trust and o-bey. }
tear Can a-bide while we trust and o-bey. } Trust and o-bey, For there's
cross, But is blest if we trust and o-bey. }

no oth-er way To be hap-py in Je-sus But to trust and o-bey.

4 But we never can prove
   The delights of his love
Until all on the altar we lay,
   For the favor he shows,
   And the joy he bestows,
Are for all who will trust and obey.

5 Then in fellowship sweet
   We will sit at his feet,
Or we'll walk by his side in the way;
   What he says we will do,
   Where he sends we will go,
Never fear, only trust and obey.

.107. HE WAITS WITH OUTSTRETCHED HANDS.

C. A. M.

C. Austin Miles.

DUET.

1. For you, sinner, for you The Saviour came to earth, And
2. For you, sinner, for you He died on Cal-va - ry; To
3. For you, sinner, for you The crown of thorns he wore, And

walked with wearied footsteps With those of humble birth. No load for him too
purchase your redemp-tion He hung upon the tree. His life he free-ly
on the cross suspend- ed, Your sins he freely bore. No word of condem-

heav - y, No path for him too steep; He came to cheer the hopeless
of-fered, Forsook his heav'nly home, And with his dy - ing whisper
na - tion Escaped his lips so true; By men he was re-ject-ed;

CHORUS.

And mourn with those that weep.)
He gent- ly bids you come. } He waits, he waits, with outstretched hands,
Will you reject him, too?)   He waits, he waits,
                                O come, O come, no more withstand
                                   O come, O come,

1.   2.

To give, to give you pardon free; :|| His gentle voice, his earnest plea.
   To give, to give

No. 108. I NEED THEE, LORD.

ELISHA A. HOFFMAN.   CHAS. EDW. PRIOR.

1. When cherished joys have tak-en wing, And sor-row wounds me
2. When sin dis-turbs my ho-ly peace, And leaves my soul in
3. When longs my soul for deep-er rest, To be with all thy
4. When strong tempta-tions me as-sail, And o'er my will al-
5. I need thee, dear-est Lord, just now While at thy throne of

with its sting, Then to thy cross for help I cling, For
sore dis-tress, To be re-stored to hap-pi-ness, I
full-ness blest, To be of per-fect peace pos-sessed, Oh,
most pre-vail, Lest faith and cour-age then should fail, I
grace I bow; To help me pay to thee my vow, I

CHORUS.

then   I need thee, Lord! ⎫
need thee, pre-cious Lord. ⎪
then   I need thee, Lord. ⎬ I need thee, precious Lord! I have no
need thee, gra-cious Lord. ⎪
need thee, my dear Lord. ⎭

help be-side; In ev-'ry time of need, Dear Christ, with me a-bide!

No. 109. LET JESUS COME INTO YOUR HEART.

C. H. M.   Mrs. C. H. Morris.

1. If you are tired of the load of your sin, Let Jesus come in-to your heart;
2. If 'tis for pur-i-ty now that you sigh, Let Jesus come in-to your heart;
3. If there's a tempest your voice cannot still, Let Jesus come in-to your heart;
4. If friends, once trusted, have proven untrue, Let Jesus come in-to your heart;
5. If you would join the glad songs of the blest, Let Jesus come in-to your heart;

If you desire a new life to be-gin, Let Je-sus come in-to your heart.
Fountains for cleansing are flowing near by, Let Je-sus come in-to your heart.
If there's a void this world never can fill, Let Je-sus come in-to your heart.
Find what a Friend he will be unto you, Let Je-sus come in-to your heart.
If you would enter the mansions of rest, Let Je-sus come in-to your heart.

CHORUS.

Just now, your doubtings give o'er; Just now, re-ject him no more;
Just now, my doubtings are o'er; Just now, re-ject-ing no more;

Just now, throw o-pen the door; Let Je-sus come in-to your heart.
Just now, I o-pen the door And Jesus comes into my heart.

No. 110. HE SAVES ME.

J. W. VAN DE VENTER.

W. S. WEEDEN.

1. The dear lov - ing Sav-iour hath found me, And shattered the fet- ters that
2. He sought me so long ere I knew him, But fi - nal - ly win-ning me
3. I nev - er, no, nev - er will leave him, Grow wea-ry of serv - ice and

bound me, Tho' all was con- fu - sion a - round me, He came and spake
to him, I yield-ed my all to pur - sue him, And asked to be
grieve him, I'll con-stant-ly trust and be - lieve him, Re-main in his

peace to my soul; The bless- ed Re-deem- er that bought me, In
filled with his grace; Al - though a vile sin - ner be - fore him, Thro'
pres-ence di - vine; A - bid-ing in love ev - er flow - ing, In

ten- der- ness con-stant- ly sought me, The way of sal - va - tion He
faith I was led to im - plore him, And now I re - joice and a -
knowledge and grace ev - er grow-ing, Con - fid- ing im - plic - it - ly,

CHORUS.

taught me, And made my heart per- fect - ly whole.
dore him, Re- stored to his lov- ing em - brace.   } He saves me, he
know- ing, That Je - sus the Sav-iour is mine.

HE SAVES ME.—Concluded.

saves me, His love fills my soul, halle-lu - jah! Oh, glo - ry, oh, glo - ry,

1. His spir - it a - bid - eth with-in ; :|| *2.* His blood cleanseth me from all sin. *Rit.*

No. 111.   I NEED THEE EVERY HOUR.

Mrs. ANNIE S. HAWKS.   Rev. R. LOWRY.

1. I need thee ev-'ry hour, Most gra - cious Lord; No ten - der voice like thine
2. I need thee ev-'ry hour; Stay thou near by; Temptations lose their pow'r
3. I need thee ev-'ry hour, Teach me thy will; And thy rich promis - es
4. I need thee ev-'ry hour, Most Ho - ly One; O make me thine in-deed,

REFRAIN.

Can peace af - ford.
When thou art nigh.
In me ful - fill.
Thou bless- ed Son.

I need thee, O,   I need thee; Ev - 'ry hour I

need thee; O bless me now, my Sav - iour! I   come to   thee.

Copyright, 1872, by R. Lowry. By per.

No. 112.   WOULD YOU SHINE FOR JESUS?

G. M. BILLS.   M. L. McPHAIL.

1. Would you shine for Je-sus? Let his love im-part   Ardor to your ac-tions,
2. Would you shine for Je-sus 'Mid the careless throng? Im-i-tate his grac-es
3. Would you shine for Je-sus As a mir-ror true? Image forth his goodness

Comfort to your heart; With your soul illumined   By the Spir-it's glow,
As you pass a-long; Make no weak surren-der   To the coarse and vile;
As revealed in you. If you thus re-flect him   Till this life is o'er,

S: FINE.   CHORUS.

You will be a bea con In this world of woe.   Shin - ing for
Keep your tongue from evil, And your lips from guile.
You will in his kingdom Shine for ev - er - more.

Shining for Je-sus, Yes,

D. S.—To the sad and err-ing, Thus for Je-sus shine.

Je - sus, Bringing light di-vine   To the sad and err-ing, Thus for

shin-ing for Je-sus,

Je-sus shine; Shin - ing for Je - sus, Bringing light divine

Shining for Je-sus, Yes, shining for Je-sus,

D.S.

WHISP'RING IN MY HEART.

J. B. M.

J. B. MACKAY.

1. Jesus found me wand'ring, Far from him astray, Tender- ly he led me
2. I can hear him whisper, When my soul is tried, "Fear not, I am with thee;
3. Would you hear the Saviour's Gentle voice within? Now, while he is calling,

To the shining way; Words of peace he whispered, Bade my fears depart;
I am at thy side." When the foe as - sails me, Je- sus takes my part;
Leave the path of sin. Peace that passeth knowledge Freely he'll im- part;

Chorus.

Oh, 'twas sweet to hear him Whisp'ring in my heart.
I rejoice to hear him Whisp'ring in my heart. } Whisp'ring, whisp'ring.
You to-day may hear him Whisp'ring in your heart.

Oh, what joy is mine; Whisp'ring, whisp'ring, Words of love divine. No strain of earthly

music Such rapture can impart; I'm glad I ever heard him Whisp'ring in my heart.

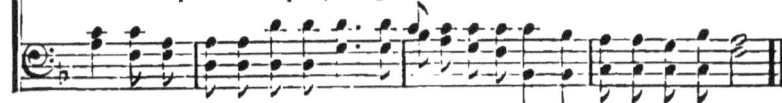

No. 114. SEEDS OF PROMISE.

JESSIE H. BROWN.

FRED. A. FILLMORE

1. Oh, scat-ter seeds of lov-ing deeds A - long the fer - tile field;
2. Tho' sown in tears thro' wea - ry years, The seed will sure - ly live;
3. The harvest-home of God will come, And af - ter toil and care,

For grain will grow from what you sow, And fruit-ful har- vest yield.
Tho' great the cost, it is not lost, For God will fruit-age give.
With joy un-told your sheaves of gold, Will all be garnered there.

CHORUS.

Then day by day.............. a-long your way............... The seeds of
Then day by day   a-long your way

prom - - ise cast, ...That ripened grain,...... from hill and
The seeds of promise cast, the seeds of promise cast,   That ripened grain,

plain,............. Be gathered home............ at last...............
from hill and plain,   Be gathered home at last, be gathered home at last.

Be gathered home at last...............

ETERNITY IS NEAR.

J. W. VanDeVenter.　　　　　　　　　　　　　　　W. S. Weeden.

Duet.

1. I see the days glide down the West, The seasons come and go ; The
2. I leave this sad and lone-ly place, But leave it all in vain, For
3. I see the fair-est flow-ers fade, The ros-y cheek grow pale ; The

dear ones laid a-way to rest　Be-neath the win-ter snow.　I
when I see the furrowed face　I hear the voice a-gain　Re-
aw-ful wreck dis-ease has made, The strongest mor-tals fail.　They

hear, while standing near their bed　So lone-ly, cold and drear,　A
ech-o from beneath the sod, "Why waste your moments here? Pre-
al-so speak to me of death　In language strong and clear ; Thy

Quartet.

voice resounding from the dead, "Eter-ni-ty is near, e-ter-ni-ty is near."
pare, prepare to meet thy God! "Eter-ni-ty is near, e-ter-ni-ty is near."
life is going with each breath　Eter-ni-ty is near, e-ter-ni-ty is near.

No. 116. JESUS LIVES.

Rev. John R. Colgan. A. F. Myers.

1. Might-y ar-my of the young, Lift the voice in cheer-ful song,
2. Tongues of chil-dren light and free, Tongues of youth all full of glee,
3. Je-sus lives, O bless-ed words! King of kings, and Lord of lords!

Send the welcome word a-long, Je-sus lives! Once he died for you and me,
Sing to all on land and sea, Je-sus lives! Light for you and all mankind,
Lift the cross and sheathe the swords, Je-sus lives! See, he breaks the pris-on wall,

Bore our sins up-on the tree, Now he lives to make us free, Je-sus lives!
Sight for all by sin made blind, Life in Je-sus all may find, Je-sus lives!
Throws a-side the dreadful pall, Conquers death at once for all, Je-sus lives!

CHORUS.

Wait not till the shadows lengthen, till you old-er grow, Ral-ly now and
Wait not Sing,

Wait not, wait, not, Sing for

sing for Je-sus, ev-'ry where you go, Lift your joy-ful voic-es high,
sing,

Je - sus,

JESUS LIVES.—Concluded.

Repeat Chorus pp.
f Rit.

Ring-ing clear thro' earth and sky, Let the blessed tidings fly, *Je-sus lives!*

No. 117.   I AM THINE, O LORD.

"Let us draw near with a true heart."—Heb. 10: 22.

FANNY J. CROSBY.   W. H. DOANE.

1. I am thine, O Lord, I have heard thy voice, And it told thy love to me;
2. Con-se-crate me now to thy service, Lord, By the pow'r of grace divine;
3. O the pure de-light of a sin-gle hour That before thy throne I spend
4. There are depths of love that I cannot know Till I cross the narrow sea,

But I long to rise in the arms of faith, And be clos-er drawn to thee.
Let my soul look up with a steadfast hope, And my will be lost in thine.
When I kneel in pray'r, and with thee my God, I commune as friend with friend.
There are heights of joy that I may not reach Till I rest in peace with thee.

REFRAIN.

Draw me near - er, nearer, blessed Lord, To the cross where thou hast died;
near - er, near - er,

Draw me near-er, nearer, nearer blessed Lord, To thy precious, bleeding side.

No. 118.

HE'S THE ONE.

J. B. M.

J. B. MACKAY.

1. Is there an - y - one can help us, one who understands our hearts, When the
2. Is there an - y - one can help us when the load is hard to bear, And we
3. Is there an - y - one can help us who can give a sinner peace, When his
4. Is there an - y - one can help us, when the end is draw-ing near, Who will

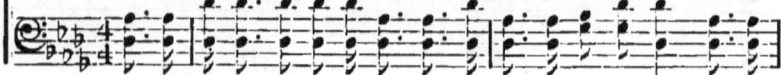

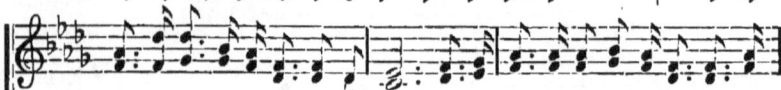

thorns of life have pierced them till they bleed ; One who sympathizes with us, who in
faint and fall beneath it in a- larm ; Who in tenderness will lift us, and the
heart is burdened down with pain and woe ; Who can speak the word of pardon that af-
go thro' death's dark waters by our side ; Who will light the way before us, and dis-

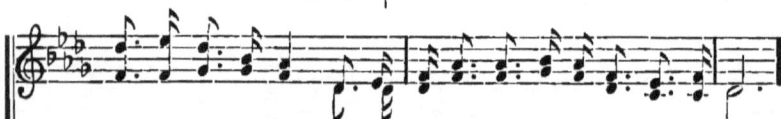

wondrous love imparts Just the ver - y, ver - y blessing that we need?
heav - y bur-den share, And sup-port us with an ev - er - last - ing arm?
fords a sweet re-lease, And whose blood can wash and make us white as snow?
pel all doubt and fear, And will bear our spir - its safe-ly o'er the tide?

CHORUS.

Yes, there's One, on-ly One, The blessed, blessed Jesus, he's the One ; When af-
Yes, there's One, only One,

flictions press the soul, when waves of trouble roll, And you need a friend to help you, he's the One.

BRIGHTEN THE WAY WITH A SMILE.

W. C. MARTIN.   J. LINCOLN HALL.

1. There are hearts that are droop-ing in sor-row to-day; There are
2. There are bur-dens most grievous and heav-y to bear; There are
3. When the soul is in dark-ness and wea-ry with care Comes the
4. O, the beau-ti-ful dawn-ing of day is not far, And the

souls un-der shad-ow, the while. O, the com-fort from God you can
souls whom the sin-ful re-vile; You can lov-ing-ly whis-per God's
temp-ter al-lur-ing with guile. You should shine in that life like the
gloaming will lin-ger a while. Let us glow like the glit-ter-ing,

CHORUS.

gen-tly con-vey, And brighten the way with a smile. ⎫
prom-is-es rare, And brighten the way with a smile. ⎪ O, brighten the
sunbeams so fair, And brighten the way with a smile. ⎬
bright morning star, And brighten the way with a smile. ⎭

way with a smile,   Yes, brighten the way with a smile,   Some
       with a smile,   with a smile,

one's drearest days you can gently beguile, And brighten the way with a smile.

HE IS THE SAVIOUR FOR ME.

E. E. HEWITT.

HOWARD E. SMITH.

1. One who will freely for-give all my sin, He is the Saviour for me;
2. One who can turn bitter waters to sweet, He is the Saviour for me;
3. One who is lov-ing and tender and true, He is the Saviour for me;

Bringing His precious salvation within, He is the Saviour for me.
Peace, "perfect peace," as I wait at His feet, He is the Saviour for me.
Able my courage and strength to renew, He is the Saviour for me.

Spread-ing His mer-cy, like sunshine, a-round, Wonder-ful grace that will
Cleans-ing me, keep-ing me, day af-ter day, Helping me walk in His
Lift-ing me up as His cross I shall bear, Calling me ev-er to

"much more a-bound;" Just such a Sav-iour in Je-sus I've found,
roy-al high-way, Hear-ing and answ'ring as hum-bly I pray,
heights pure and fair, In His great har-vest-ing, let-ting me share,

CHORUS.

He is the Sav-iour for me.)
He is the Sav-iour for me. }   He is the Sav-iour for
He is the Sav-iour for me.)
                     for me;

HE IS THE SAVIOUR FOR ME.—Concluded.

me; (for me;) Glo - ry to him ev - er be; Just such a

Saviour in Je - sus I've found, He is the Saviour for me. (for me.)

No. 121. IN THE HOUR OF TRIAL.

JAMES MONTGOMERY.   SPENCER LANE.

1. In the hour of tri - al, Jesus, plead for me ; Lest by base de-ni - al
2. With forbidden pleasures Would this vain world charm; Or its sordid treasures
3. Should thy mercy send me Sorrow, toil and woe ; Or should pain attend me
4. When my last hour cometh, Fraught with strife and pain, When my dust returneth

I depart from thee, When thou see'st me wav - er, With a look re-
Spread to work me harm ; Bring to my re- membrance Sad Gethsem-a-
On my path be - low: Grant that I may nev - er Fail thy hand to
To the dust a - gain; On thy truth re - ly - ing, Thro' that mortal

call,   Nor for fear nor fa - vor   Suf- fer me to fall.
ne,   Or, in dark - er   semblance, Cross-crown'd Calva- ry.
see ;   Grant that I may ev - er   Cast my care on thee.
strife,   Je - sus, take me, dy - ing,   To e - ter - nal life.

MY LORD, TO THEE.

FLORA KIRKLAND.   W. C. WEEDEN.

1. From the country of sor-row and sin Comes the prod-i-gal,
2. While he wandered and suffered and sinned, For his coming that
3. In the sor-row-ful country of sin, 'Mid its husks and its
4. O re-turn to thy Father to-day, For he loves thee with

mourning the past, And the love of the father shines forth, And the
father had yearned; And the robe and the ring and the feast Are pre-
vain, fleeting show, Precious souls in their wilfulness stray From the
love all un-told, And a robe and a crown thou shalt wear At the

CHORUS.

son finds a refuge at last.
pared, for the son hath returned!
Father who loveth them so.
feast in the cit-y of gold.

Coming to thee, com-ing, Coming, my

Lord, to thee; Coming to thee, com-ing, Coming, my Lord, to thee.

FOOTSTEPS OF JESUS.

Mary B. C. Slade. A. B. Everett.

1. Sweet-ly, Lord, have we heard thee call-ing, Come, fol-low me!
2. Tho' they lead o'er the cold, dark mountains, Seek-ing his sheep;
3. If they lead through the tem-ple ho-ly, Preach-ing the word;

And we see where thy footprints fall-ing, Lead us to thee.
Or a-long by Si-lo-am's fountains, Help-ing the weak.
Or in homes of the poor and low-ly, Serv-ing the Lord.

Chorus.

Foot-prints of Je-sus, that make the path-way glow;

We will fol-low the steps of Je-sus wher-e'er they go.

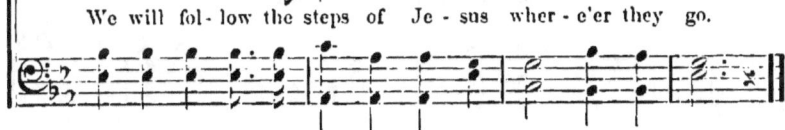

4 Tho', dear Lord, in thy pathway keeping,
   We follow thee;
 Thro' the gloom of that place of weeping,
   Gethsemane!

5 If thy way and its sorrows bearing,
   We go again,
 Up the slope of the hillside, bearing
   Our cross of pain.

6 By and by, through the shining portals,
   Turning our feet,
 We shall walk with the glad immortals,
   Heaven's golden streets.

7 Then at last, when on high he sees us,
   Our journey done,
 We will rest where the steps of Jesus
   End at his throne.

No. 124. IN THE PALACE OF THE KING.

C. A. M.

C. Austin Miles.

1. There's a mansion that is waiting o - ver there, 'Tis a mansion which my
2. Soon as ransomed we'll be gathered on the shore, From our loved ones we'll be
3. Though temptations oft assail me, I'll not fear, For I feel that my trans-

over there,

Saviour will pre - pare ; And though dark the way, and dreary, I'll press
part - ed nev - er - more ; We will shout the glad "Hosanna !" And march
la - tion must be near ; Just a few more years of waiting, Then I'll

will prepare ;

D. S.—Of the precious blood of Je - sus, Our re-

Fine. Chorus.

onward, while I sing Of the palace of the King.
upward, while we sing, To the palace of the King. } We will shout, we will sing,
fly on "Joyful Wing" To the palace of the King.

demption purchasing, In the palace of the King.

D. S.

How our voic- es will ring, As we tell the blessed sto- ry ev - er new ;

ever new;

No. 125. THE WONDERFUL STORY.

C. H. G.

Chas. H. Gabriel.

1. O sweet is the story of Je-sus, The won-derful Saviour of
2. He came from the brightest of glo-ry; His blood as a ransom he
3. His mer-cy flows on like a riv-er, His love is unmeasured and

men, Who suf-fered and died for the sin-ner—I'll tell it a-
gave, To pur-chase e-ternal redemption, And oh, he is
free; His grace is for-ev-er suf-fi-cient, It reach-es and

Chorus.

gain and a-gain! \
mighty to save! } O won - derful, wonderful sto - ry, The
pu-ri-fies me. / O wonderful sto - ry, O wonderful story, The

dear - est that ev-er was told;..... I'll repeat it in glo - ry, The
dearest that ev - er, that ever was told; I'll repeat it in

rit.

wonderful sto - ry, Where I........... shall his beauty be - hold.....
glory, The wonderful story, Where I shall his beau - ty, his beauty behold.

No. 126. **CHRIST IS THE CONQUEROR.**

Irvin H. Mack.   J. Lincoln Hall.

1. The Sav - iour leads His faith - ful on To bat - tle for the right;
2. Be - fore them is the prec-ious cross; They glo - ry in its fame;
3. Their tongues the name of Je - sus sounds; The name they love so well.

Their mot - to is "Thy will be done," The hosts of sin they'll smite.
It lifts their thoughts from earth-ly dross, To think of Je - sus' name.
With - in their hearts His love abounds; For - ev - er there to dwell.

No fears a - larm, no ter - rors stop, They go with stead - y tread;
From con - quest un - to vic - to - ry, Press forth the might - y throng;
O who will join this bright ar - ray. This arm - y of the Lord?

And none shall by the way - side drop, For Christ is at the head.
The hosts of Sa - tan all must flee, Be - fore the vic - tor's song.
O who will now the call o - bey, Be gov - erned by his word?

Chorus.

Christ   is the con - quer - or, Christ   is the con - quer - or,

CHRIST IS THE CONQUEROR. Concluded.

O glo - ri - ous con - quer-or, Who leads to vic - to - ry.

No. 127.
J. W. VanDeVenter. **I SURRENDER ALL.** W. S. Weeden.

Solo.

1. { All to Je-sus I sur-ren-der, All to him I free-ly give; }
   { I will ev-er love and trust him, In his presence dai-ly live. }
2. { All to Je-sus I sur-ren-der, Humbly at his feet I bow; }
   { Worldly pleasures all for-sak-en, Take me, Je-sus, take me now. }
3. { All to Je-sus I sur-ren-der, Make me, Saviour, whol-ly thine; }
   { Let me feel the Ho-ly Spir-it, Tru-ly know that thou art mine. }

Chorus.

I sur-ren-der all, I sur-ren-der all;
I surrender all, I surrender all;

All to thee, my bless-ed Sav-iour, I sur-ren-der all.

4 All to Jesus I surrender,
Lord, I give myself to thee;
Fill me with thy love and power,
Let thy blessing fall on me.

5 All to Jesus I surrender,
Now I feel the sacred flame;
O the joy of full salvation!
Glory, glory to his name!

No. 128. I'LL GO WHERE YOU WANT ME TO GO.

MARY BROWN.   CONSECRATION.   CARRIE E. ROUNSEFELL.

Andante.

1. It may not be on the mountain's height, Or o-ver the stormy sea;
2. Perhaps to-day there are lov-ing words Which Jesus would have me speak—
3. There's sure-ly somewhere a low-ly place, In earth's harvest fields so wide—

It may not be at the bat-tle's front My Lord will have need of me;
There may be now in the paths of sin Some wand'rer whom I should seek—
Where I may la-bor thro' life's short day For Je-sus the cru-ci-fied—

But if by a still, small voice he calls To paths that I do not know,
O Sav-iour, if thou wilt be my guide, Tho' dark and rug-ged the way,
So trust-ing my all to thy ten-der care, And knowing thou lov-est me,

S: FINE.

I'll answer, dear Lord, with my hand in thine, I'll go where you want me to go.
My voice shall ech-o the message sweet, I'll say what you want me to say.
I'll do thy will with a heart sincere, I'll be what you want me to be.

D. S.—I'll say what you want me to say, dear Lord, I'll be what you want me to be.

REFRAIN.   *D S.*

I'll go where you want me to go, dear Lord, Over mountain, or plain, or sea;

No. 129. "BRING YE ALL THE TITHES."

HELEN E. RASMUSSEN.   Mal. 3: 10.   H. L. GILMOUR.

1. Hear the words of scripture from the a - ges past, "Bring ye all the
2. Do you seek to know the Ho - ly Spir-it's power? "Bring ye all the
3. Is there aught that stands between you and your Lord? "Bring ye all the
4. Lift your heart this moment : claim him Lord and King, As ye bring the
5. Let the anthems roll in grandeur thro' the skies, Having brought the

tithes into the storehouse," Make a con - se-cra-tion that will ev - er last,
tithes into the storehouse." Live in sweet communion with him hour by hour,
tithes into the storehouse." Bring them on con-ditions promised in his word,
tithes into the storehouse. Trust the blessed promise, and your praise shall ring,
tithes into the storehouse; Joy - ous hal - le-lu-jah's from our hearts a-rise

CHORUS.

Trusting for the promised bless - ing.
While he gives the promised bless - ing. "Bring ye all the tithes in-to the
And he'll pour you out a bless - ing.
From the heart he is pos - sess - ing.
For we have the promised bless - ing.

storehouse, And prove me now saith the Lord of hosts; And I will pour you

out a bless - ing, There shall not be room enough to re - ceive it."

No. 130. THE LORD IS MY SHEPHERD.

T. KOSCHAT.

Lento.

1. The Lord is my Shep-herd, no want shall I know, I feed in green pas-tures, safe fold-ed I rest; He lead-eth my soul where the still wa-ters flow, Re - stores me when wand'ring, re - deems when oppress'd, Re - stores me when wand'ring, redeems when oppressed.

2. Thro' the val - ley and shad-ow of death tho' I stray, Since thou art my Guardian, no e - vil I fear; Thy rod shall de - fend me, thy staff be my stay; No harm can be - fall, with my Com-fort - er near, No harm can be - fall, with my Com-fort-er near.

3. In the midst of af - flic-tion my ta - ble is spread; With bless-ings un - meas-ured my cup run-neth o'er; With per-fume and oil thou a - noint-est my head; Oh, what shall I ask of thy prov - i - dence more? Oh, what shall I ask of thy prov-i-dence more.

4. Let good - ness and mer - cy, my boun-ti - ful God, Still fol - low my steps till I meet thee a - bove. I seek by the path which my fore - fa - thers trod, Thro' the land of their so-journ, thy king-dom of love, Thro' the land of their so-journ, thy kingdom of love.

No. 131. HIDING, SAFELY HIDING.

E. O. E. and A. B.

E. O. EXCELL.

1. 'Neath the shad-ow of th' Almighty, In the presence of my King;
2. When the storms of life are rag-ing, Clos-er to his side I cling:
3. All my life, my love, my service, All I have to him I bring;

I am hid - ing, hid - ing, Hiding in the shadow of his wing.
I am hiding, safely hiding, hiding, safely hiding,

In the se - cret place a - bid-ing, In con - tentment I can sing.
In his love I'm safe - ly sheltered, Peace and qui - et he doth bring.
He will hide me, safe - ly hide me Till in heav'n this song I sing:

FINE.

I am hid - ing, hid - ing, Hiding in the shadow of his wing.
I am hiding, safely hiding, hiding, safely hiding,

REFRAIN.

D.S.

Hid - ing, hid - ing, Hiding in the shadow of his wing.
Hiding, safely hiding, hiding, safely hiding,   I'm hiding, hiding.

No. 132.   COME TO ME.

Rev. JOHNSON OATMAN, Jr.

GEO. F. ROSCHE.

1. Wea - ry soul, why art thou so distressed? Come where there is
2. "Bring to me thy heav-y load of sin, On the cross I
3. "Come to me; tho' all is dark as night; I will make thy
4. "Come to me!" O hear him call-ing "Come, Come to me, O

per-fect peace and rest, Lean up - on thy lov-ing Saviour's breast;
died thy soul to win, Come to me, and I will take thee in."
pathway clear and bright, Come to me, and I will be thy light,
child no lon-ger roam, Leave the path of dan-ger, death and gloom,

CHORUS.

In his love thou shalt be ful - ly blest.
Ho - ly Spir - it, now the work be - gin.
Walk with me in faith, and not by sight."
Come to me, and I will lead thee home.

"Come to me," O hear the Saviour call to thee, "I'll sus-tain, tho' trials of life may fall to thee."

"Come to me," O hear the Saviour call, "Come to me, I will be all in all."

No. 133.   I WOULD KNOW THEE.

ALFRED A. HOLT.

Dedicated to Trinity Baptist Church, Camden, N. J.

W. S. WEEDEN.

DUET.

1. Precious Saviour, I would know thee, Wilt thou not thyself re- veal?
2. Tho' the cross be heav - y, Saviour, Thou didst bear the cross for me;
3. All to thee I now sur - ren- der, Take my heart, my life, my all;
4. May the bless - ed Ho - ly Spir - it Fill this longing heart of mine;

Fill my soul this ver - y mo- ment, Let me now thy presence feel.
Thou hast saved me, yes, and kept me, Let me bear the cross for thee.
O ac- cept me, tho' unworth - y, As be - fore thee now I fall.
Fill it now to o - ver- flow- ing, And the glo - ry shall be thine.

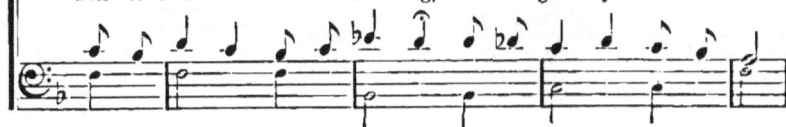

CHORUS.

I would know thee, blessed Sav - iour, Ev - er trust thee, and o - bey ;

Lead, O lead me ; I will fol - low, Fol- low close - ly all the way.

JESUS FOREVER FOR ME.

C. A. M.

C. Austin Miles.

1. Trust-ing in Je - sus from day to day, Bright-ens each step of the
2. Com-fort in suf-fer-ing and dis-tress, Lead - er and Guide in the
3. Know-ing that Je - sus is at my side, I will not fal - ter what-
4. Pass-ing thro' Jor-dan to Glo - ry Land, Join - ing in songs with the

drear - y way; When in the dark - ness no light I see—
wil - der - ness; Ev - er re - main-ing when oth - ers flee,
e'er be - tide; Liv - ing or dy - ing my song shall be,
an - gel band; This be my mot - to e - ter - nal - ly,

CHORUS.

Je - sus for-ev-er for me. Je - - sus for-
Je - sus for - ev - er, yes,

ev - - er, for - ev - - er for me;............
Je - sus for me, Yes, Je - sus for - ev - er, yes, Je - sus for me;

Dai - - ly I'm sing-ing, Je - sus for-ev-er for me......
Dai - ly, yes, dai - ly I'm sing-ing, Je - sus for - ev - er for me, for me.

No. 135.

FOR ME.

"He careth for you."—I Peter 5: 7.

FLORA KIRKLAND.   W. S. WEEDEN.

1. For me, for me, this ho-ly calm! For me, for me, this precious balm!
2. I'll cast my bur-dens on the Lord, I'll rest up-on his gracious word;
3. My Saviour cares, my Saviour cares, My wounds he heals, my home prepares,

This per-fect free-dom from despair, This blessed truth,—"my Lord doth care."
I'll cast my ev-'ry care on him, And find a joy, no tears can dim.
My strength restores, my burden bears, Oh, blessed thought! "my Saviour cares!"

CHORUS.

My Saviour cares,............ my Saviour cares,............ He sees my
(My Saviour cares,   my Saviour cares,)

tears........... my woes he shares;.......... My Saviour cares,...........my Saviour
(He sees my tears,   my woes he shares;   My Saviour cares,)

ritard.

cares!............. I *rest content;*............. my Saviour cares,...........
(my Saviour cares   I'll rest content;)   (my Saviour cares.)

No. 136. ONE MORE DAY'S WORK FOR JESUS.

"I must work the works of him that sent me, while it is day."—John 9: 4.

Miss Anna Warner.

Rev. Robert Lowry, by per.

1. One more day's work for Je - sus; One less of life for
2. One more day's work for Je - sus; How glo - rious is my
3. One more day's work for Je - sus; How sweet the work has
4. One more day's work for Je - sus— Oh, yes, a wea - ry
5. Oh, bless - ed work for Je - sus! Oh, rest at Je - sus'

me! But heav'n is near - er, And Christ is dear - er, Than
King! 'Tis joy, not du - ty, To speak his beau - ty, My
been, To tell the sto - ry, To show the glo - ry, When
day; But heav'n shines clear - er, And rest comes near - er, At
feet! There toil seems pleas - ure. My wants are treas - ure, And

yes - ter-day to me; His love and light Fill all my soul to-night.
soul mounts on the wing At the mere tho't How Christ my life has bought.
Christ's flock en-ter in! How it did shine In this poor heart of mine.
each step of the way; And Christ in all— Be-fore his face I fall.
pain for him is sweet, Lord, if I may, I'll serve an-oth - er day.

CHORUS.

One more day's work for Je - sus, One more day's work for
Je - sus, One more day's work for Jesus, One less of life for me.

THE PLACE CALLED CALVARY.

E. E. Hewitt.   Howard E. Smith.

1. O thou bleeding Lamb of God, Thou the path   of death hast trod,
2. Flowing here the   crimson tide, Fount of bless - ing deep and wide,
3. O the cru - el   pain he bore, When the crown of thorns he wore ;
4. Come, oh, come, for he'll re- ceive All who on   his   name be- lieve ;

Pouring out   thy life for me,   At   the place called Cal - va - ry.
Saviour, wash a - way my sin,   Bring thy cleansing power with- in.
Sin- ner, come ; for you and me   Je - sus died on   Cal - va - ry.
Find sal- va - tion full and free, At the place called Cal - va - ry.

Chorus.

Wonderful place called Cal- va - ry,   Wonderful place called Cal- va - ry ;
        called Cal - va- ry.   called Cal - va - ry ;

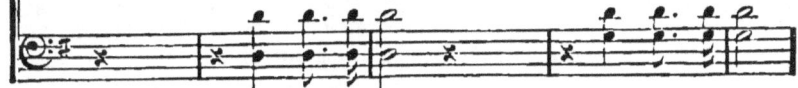

Love, redeem - ing love, I see,   At the place called Cal - va - ry.

No. 138. WE SHALL SHINE AS THE STARS.

J. W. V.

J. W. Van De Venter.

DUET. ALTO & TENOR.

1. We may tar - ry a-while here as stran - gers, Un - no - ticed by
2. We may nev - er be rich in earth's treas - ure, Nor rise on the
3. We may live in a tent or a cot - tage, And die in se -
4. We may sleep 'neath the clods of the val - ley, Our bod - ies may

those who pass by; But the Sav-iour will crown us in glo - ry,
lad - der of fame; But the saints will at last be re - ward - ed,
clu - sion un - known, But the Fa-ther who seeth in se - cret,
crum-ble to dust, But the Sav-iour will raise us im - mor - tal,

CHORUS.

To shine as the stars of the sky. ⎫
Made rich in Em-man - u - el's name. ⎪
Re - mem - bers each one of his own. ⎬ We shall shine as the
To reap the re - ward of the just. ⎭

stars of the morn- ing, With Je - sus the cru - ci - fied one; We shall

rise to be like him for - ev - er, E - ter - nal-ly shine as the sun.

No. 139. HOW CAN I SERVE THEE BEST?

FLORA KIRKLAND.

CHAS. H. GABRIEL.

1. Where shall I go, Lord, where shall I go? Wisdom to guide me thou wilt bestow;
2. What shall I say, Lord, what shall I say? Thou art my Teacher, *teach* me to-day;
3. What shall I read, Lord, what shall I read; Here thy protection ev-er I need;
4. Purchas'd by thee, Lord, now I am thine, Time, thought and effort nevermore mine;

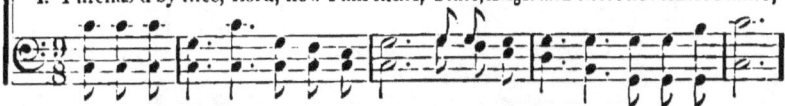

Help me to go, Lord, where thou dost lead, Trusting thy promise, "Grace for all need."
On-ly and ev - er help me to be Speaking for thee, Lord, speaking for thee.
Led by thy Spir- it sent from a- bove, E'en thro' temptation safely I'll move.
Thou hast redeem'd me, help me to be Shining for thee, Lord, on- *ly* for thee.

CHORUS.

What shall it be, ... Lord, what shall it be?
What shall it be, what shall it be?

How can I serve thee, serve thee best? Speak un - to
How can I serve thee, serve thee best?

me, Lord, speak un- to me, Help me to shrink from no test.

Copyright, 1899 by W. S. Weeden.

No. 140. HOLY, HOLY! LORD GOD ALMIGHTY!

"They rest not day nor night, saying, Holy, Holy, Holy, Lord God Almighty, which was, and is, and is to come."—Rev. 4: 8.

REGINALD HEBER, D.D.   Rev. J. B. DYKES.

1. Ho-ly, ho-ly, ho-ly! Lord God Almight-y! Ear-ly in the
2. Ho-ly, ho-ly, ho-ly! all the saints a-dore thee, Casting down their
3. Ho-ly, ho-ly, ho-ly! tho' the darkness hide thee, Tho' the eye of
4. Ho-ly, ho-ly, ho-ly! Lord God Almight-y! All thy works shall

morn-ing our song shall rise to thee; Ho-ly, ho-ly, ho-ly!
gold-en crowns around the glass-y sea; Cher-u-bim and ser-a-phim
sin-ful man thy glo-ry may not see; On-ly thou art ho-ly,
praise thy name in earth, and sky, and sea; Ho-ly, ho-ly, ho-ly,

Mer-ci-ful and Mighty, God in three persons, blessed Trini-ty!
falling down before thee, Which wert, and art, and evermore shalt be.
there is none beside thee, Per-fect in pow'r, in love, and puri-ty.
Mer-ci-ful and Mighty, God in three persons, blessed Trini-ty! A-men.

THE GRACE OF OUR LORD JESUS CHRIST.

"The grace of our Lord Jesus Christ."—Rom. 16: 24.

W. F. SHERWIN.

The grace of our Lord Je-sus Christ be with you all. A-men.

No. 141.

A SONG OF PEACE.

LIZZIE DE ARMOND.

CHAS. H. GABRIEL.

DUET.

1. O soul, be glad, and joyful sing   Loud hal- le- lujahs to your King;
2. O praise his name who turned thy night Of sorrows in- to day so bright;
3. Abounding grace in him I   see;   My life with blessings full and free

He paid the price on Calva - ry,   The debt of love to set you free.......
To him all glo- ry doth be- long;   Rejoice, my soul, and swell the song...
He daily crowns; by night, by day,   Joy in the Lord, praise him alway....

CHORUS.

O God, our hearts............ to thee we raise.............. In songs of
hearts to thee we raise,   our   hearts to thee we raise   In

O God, our hearts   to   thee   we   raise   In   songs   of

grat - - itude and praise;........ Thy voice hath spok - - en, "Peace, be
songs of gratitude, of gratitude and praise; Thy voice hath spoken, "Peace, be still," hath

grat - i - tude,   of gratitude and praise; Thy voice hath spoken, "Peace, be

still,"................ And earth and sea   o - bey   thy will..........
spoken, "Peace, be still," And earth and sea o - bey thy will,   o - bey thy will.

still,   be   still,"   And   earth   and   sea   o - bey   thy will.

No. 142. "MY TIMES ARE IN THY HAND."

FLORA KIRKLAND.

To my daughter, Mrs. F. M. Weeden-Beakes.

W. S. WEEDEN.

1. Thou knowest all a - bout me, I need not un - der - stand;
2. I do not need to tell thee, I nev - er need ex - plain;
3. O place of per - fect bless - ing! O hand once pierced for me!

Thou knowest all a - bout me, "My times are in thy hand."
Thou knowest all my mo - tives, Thou knowest all my pain.
Sweet peace my soul pos - sess - ing, My life is hid in thee.

CHORUS.

"My times are in thy hand," Lord, Thou plannest all for me;

I would not choose my path - way, I leave it all to thee.

No. 143. HAVE YE RECEIVED THE HOLY GHOST?

C. H. M.

Mrs. C. H. Morris.

1. Ye are the tem-ples, Je-sus hath spoken,   Temples of God's ho-ly
2. He who has pardoned surely will cleanse thee, All of the dross of thy
3. Showers of mer-cy, ful-ness of blessing, Ev-er the Spir-it's in-
4. Wea-ry of wand'ring, come in-to Canaan, Feast on the ful-ness and

Spir-it di-vine; Have ye received him, bidden him en-ter, Make his a-
nature re-fine; Cleansed from all sin, his Spirit will en-ter, Fill you and
dwelling at-tend; 'Tis this enduement, pow-er of service, Fruits for your
fat of the land; Feed on the man-na, dwell in the sunshine, Led by his

Chorus.

bode in that poor heart of thine?   Have...... ye received,........
thrill you with power di-vine.
la-bor he surely will send.
Spir-it and kept by his hand.   Have ye received,   have ye received,

since   ye be-lieved,   The bless-ed Ho-ly Ghost?..........
since ye believed. since ye believed, blessed, blessed Holy, blessed Holy Ghost?

He who has promised, gift of the Father, Have ye received the Holy Ghost?
received

Copyright, 1897, by H. L. Gilmour

No. 144. AS PANTETH THE HART.

Robt. L. Fletcher. I. H. Meredith.

Moderato.

1. As panteth the hart in the sultry glade, When chased from the brook and the
2. My tears are my sustenance night and day, And where is thy God? they of-
3. Why art thou disqui-et-ed, O my soul? My life shall the mercies of
4. My soul, O my God, have my foes cast down, Yet once were thy people held
5. Yet kindness and love will the Lord command, And songs in the night in an
6. The sword of my foes seeks my soul to slay, And where is thy God? hear the

cooling shade ; So, far from thy courts in captiv - i - ty, My soul is a-
fending say ; Then well I remember the for-mer days, With multitudes
God control ; Yet him will I praise, while my years prolong, The help of whose
in renown ; Deep answers, too deep when the thunders roar, So billows their
alien land ; Then why do I cry, hath my God forgot? Why mourn that op-
scoffers say ; Yet him will I praise, while my years prolong, The help of whose

Refrain.

thirst, O my God, for thee. }
throughing the house of praise.
coun - te-nance is my song. } As panteth the hart for wa-ter brooks, so
torrents up - on me pour.
pression is now my lot?
coun - te-nance is my song. }

pant - eth my soul for thee ; My soul is a - thirst,

AS PANTETH THE HART.—Concluded.

ril.

My soul is a - thirst, Thy lov - ing face to see.

No. 145. BETTER FARTHER ON.

FLORA KIRKLAND.   Arr. by W. S. WEEDEN

1. When the clouds of trouble gath- er Round the pilgrim's homeward way,
2. In the sun - ny times of blessing, When the days pass glad - ly on,
3. In the bit - ter night of sor- row, When the light of joy seems gone,
4. Through the valley of the shadow, Where the Master's feet have gone,

Fine.

Through the darkness Faith keeps singing Of a bet- ter, brighter day.
Faith points upward—"'tis a foretaste Of the glo - ry far - ther on."
Faith will whisper, "No more sorrow In the cit - y far - ther on."
Faith will sing with heav'nly rapture, "It is bet- ter far - ther on."

D.S.—Je - sus will for - sake you nev - er! It is bet- ter far - ther on."

CHORUS.   D.S.

Farther on there's bliss for- ev - er! Count the milestones one by one.

No. 146. MY FATHER KNOWS.

S. M. I. HENRY.

E. O. EXCELL.

1. I know my heav'nly Father knows............ The storms that would my
2. I know my heav'nly Father knows............ The balm I need to
3. I know my heav'nly Father knows............ How frail I am to
4. I know my heav'nly Father knows............ The hour my journey

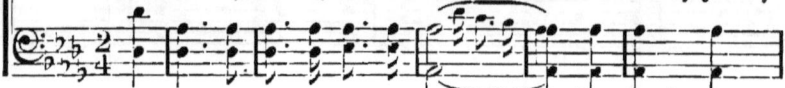

way op - pose,............ But he can drive the clouds a-
soothe my woes,............ And with his touch of love di-
meet my foes,............ But he my cause will e'er de-
here will close,............ And may that hour, O faithful

way,............ And turn my darkness in - to day,............ And
vine,............ He heals this wounded soul of mine,............ He
fend,............ Uphold and keep me to the end,............ Up-
Guide,............ Find me safe sheltered by thy side,............ Find

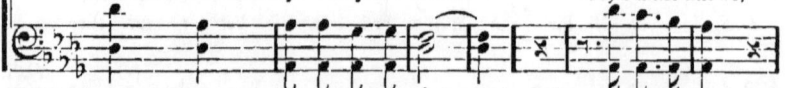

CHORUS.

turn my darkness in - to day.
heals this wounded soul of mine. } He knows,............ he
hold and keep me to the end.
me safe sheltered by thy side.

My Father knows,

knows............... The storms that would my way op - pose, He
I'm sure he knows, That would my way op - pose.

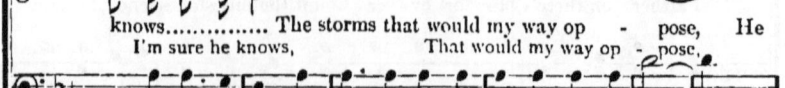

knows,.......... he knows, And tempers ev'ry wind that blows.
My Father knows, The wind that blows.

No. 147. THE HIGHER LEVEL.

Flora Kirkland. I. H. Meredith.

1. Pilgrims, trav'ling to yon cit - y, Turn to Christ your weary eyes;
2. Hath he saved you, doth he keep you? Let him have his blessed will;
3. Do you fal - ter 'neath the pressure Of some heav - y weight of care?
4. Joy is high, but peace is higher, Hope is bright, but faith is grand;

Fine.

Walk no long - er in the lowlands; To a high - er lev - el rise.
Trust his goodness; trust his wisdom; Storm or sunshine, trust him still.
Climb to-day to faith's high lev- el, You will find the Master there.
We may reach these higher lev - els, Guid - ed by the Master's hand.

D.S.—Rise to high - er heights of ser - vice; In the Master's im-age grow.

Chorus.

D.S.

Climb by faith to high- er lev- els, Leave the val - ley far be - low;

No. 148.   O 'TWAS LOVE.

A. A. Payn.

C. Austin Miles.

1. On the cross my Saviour died, Yes, for me was cru-ci- fied, Hal- le- lu-
2. From his glorious realm of light; To a world of sin-curst night, Halle - lu-

Halle-

jah! hal-le-lu-jah! He endured the sin and shame, Hallelujah! Praise his
jah! hal-le-lu - jah! Jesus came my soul to save From the terrors of the
lujah!   hallelujah!

Chorus.

name That he should die for me.
grave; Halle- lu- jah! Praise his name.
     Praise his name.

‖: O twas love that passeth under-
‖: O 'twas love, 'twas love that

1

stand - - ing, Hal- le- lu - jah! hal- le- lu - jah!:‖
passeth understanding,   Hal-le-lu-jah!   hal-le-lu-jah!:‖

2

That Christ should die for me.
        for me.

3 Was such love as this e'er known?
Was such love to mortals shown?
Hallelujah! hallelujah!
That my Lord his life would give
That my sinful soul might live!
Hallelujah! Praise his name.

4 This my daily song shall be,
Jesus Christ has died for me;
Hallelujah! hallelujah!
Though the waves about me roll,
They shall not o'erwhelm my soul;
Hallelujah! Praise his name

No. 149.
JESUS, MY SAVIOR.

J. W. Van De Venter.

1. Je - sus, my Sav - ior, Keep me ev - er near Thy side,
2. Com - fort in sor - row, In af - flic - tion be my friend;
3. Down in the val - ley Leave me not a - lone to die,

Help me to trust Thee, In Thy love a - bide; When the storms as -
Draw me still near-er, Lead me to the end; When the world for-
When time is fleet-ing, Je-sus, draw me nigh. Just a lit - tle

- sail me, And the bil-lows 'round me roll, In Thy bo - som fold me,
- sakes me, And its friendship proves untrue, In Thy ten - der mer-cy
clos - er, Near-er to Thy lov-ing breast, When we cross the riv - er

Refrain.

Hide my troubled soul.
Gent-ly lead me through. } Je - sus, my Sav-ior, Leave, oh, leave me
To the land of rest.

not a - lone, Ev - er, for - ev - er, Make Thy presence known.

No. 150.

DOING HIS WILL.

C. H. M.

Mrs. C. H. Morris.

1. Just to trust in the Lord, just to lean on his word, Just to feel I am
2. When my way darkest seems, when are blighted my dreams, Just to feel that the
3. Then my heart will be light, then my path will be bright, If I've Je - sus for

his ev-'ry day; Just to walk by his side with his Spir-it to guide, Just to
Lord knoweth best; Just to yield to his will, just to trust and be still, Just to
my dearest friend; Counting all loss but gain, such a friend to obtain, True and

Chorus.

fol - low where he leads the way.)
lean on his bos - om and rest. } Just to say what he wants me to
faith - ful he'll be to the end.)

what he

pp

say, And be still when he whispers to me;........... Just to
wants me to say, when he whispers to me;

go where he wants me to go,........... Just to be what he wants me to be.
where he wants me to go,

No. 151. THERE IS A GREEN HILL FAR AWAY.

Cecil F. Alexander.

Geo. C. Stebbins. By per.

Moderato.

1. There is a green hill far a-way, Without a cit-y wall;
2. We may not know, we can-not tell, What pains he had to bear;
3. He died that we might be forgiv'n, He died to make us good,
4. There was no oth-er good enough To pay the price of sin;

Where the dear Lord was cru-ci-fied, Who died to save us all.
But we believe it was for us He hung and suffered there.
That we might go at last to heav'n, Sav'd by his precious blood.
He on-ly could un-lock the gate Of heav'n and let us in.

Chorus.

Oh, dear-ly, dear-ly has he loved, And we must love him, too;

rit.

And trust in his re-deeming blood, And try his works to do.

No. 152.   BLESSED ASSURANCE.

"He is faithful that hath promised."—HEB. 10 : 28.

F. J. CROSBY.   MRS. JOSEPH F. KNAPP.

1. Bless-ed as - sur- ance, Je - sus is   mine!   O, what a fore- taste of
2. Per- fect sub- mis- sion, per- fect de - light,   Vis-ions of rap - ture now
3. Per- fect sub- mis- sion, all is at   rest,   I   in my Sav - iour am

glo - ry di - vine! Heir of sal - va - tion, purchase of   God,
burst on my   sight. An - gels de - scend- ing bring from a - bove,
hap - py and   blest, Watching and wait - ing, look- ing a - bove,

CHORUS.

Born of his Spir - it, wash'd in his   blood.)
Ech - oes of mer - cy, whis-pers of   love. }   This is my sto - ry,
Fill'd with his good- ness, lost in his   love.)

this is my   song, Praising my Sav-iour all the day   long;   This is my

sto - ry, this is my   song, Praising my Sav- iour all the day long.

Copyright, 1873, by Joseph F. Knapp. By per.

No. 153.　　　　BLESSED HOUR OF PRAYER.

"—went into the temple at the hour of prayer."—Acts 3: 1.

FANNY J. CROSBY.　　　　　　　　　　　　　　W. H. DOANE.

1. 'Tis the blessed hour of prayer, when our hearts lowly bend, And we
2. 'Tis the blessed hour of prayer, when the Saviour draws near, With a
3. 'Tis the blessed hour of prayer, when the tempted and tried To the
4. 'Tis the blessed hour of prayer; trusting him, we be- lieve That the

gath - er to Je - sus, our Saviour and friend; If we come to him in
ten- der com - passion his children to hear; When he tells us we may
Saviour who loves them their sorrow con- fide; With a sym - pathiz - ing
blessing we're needing we'll sure - ly receive; In the fullness of this

faith, his pro- tec- tion to share, What a balm for the wea - ry! O how
cast at his feet ev - 'ry care, What a balm for the wea - ry! O how
heart he removes ev - 'ry care; What a balm for the wea - ry! O how
trust we shall lose ev - 'ry care; What a balm for the wea - ry! O how

D. S.—What a balm for the wea - ry! O how

Fine. REFRAIN.　　　　　　　　　　　　　　　D. S.

sweet to be there! Bless-ed hour of pray'r, Blessed hour of pray'r;

No. 154.   **THE BOLTED DOOR.**

Rev. John Parker.

Wm. J. Kirkpatrick.

1. Do you know the blessed Saviour's at the door? That he lin-gers there to
2. Do not keep him longer wait-ing at the door; Hear him knocking, calling
3. Will you close your heart against him at the door? Will he not be all you
4. Oh, to think that Je-sus waits out-side the door, He may leave you, to re-

bless you more and more? Will you not in-vite him in, And his
loud - er than be - fore. Bid him wel-come now with - in, Turn a -
need for - ev - er - more? He will take a - way your pride, Be your
turn, no, nev - er - more; Soon his Spir - it may be gone, Leave you

fel - lowship be-gin, He is wait-ing, knocking, calling at the door.
way from ev - 'ry sin, He will en - ter, and the feast be ev - er - more.
nev - er-fail-ing guide, To the mansions where the blessed ones a - dore.
help-less and a-lone, Haste to hear him now and o - pen wide the door.

CHORUS.

He is wait - - ing, He is knocking at the door, He is
Waiting, he is wait-ing,   Knocking at the door,

wait - - ing, He is knocking at the door, He is wait - - ing, He is
Waiting, he is waiting,   Knocking at the door,   Waiting, he is waiting,

THE BOLTED DOOR.—Concluded.

Rit.

knocking at the door, He is waiting, he is knocking at the door.

He is knocking at the door.

No. 155.   MINE EYES SHALL BEHOLD HIM.

FANNY J. CROSBY.   WM. J. KIRKPATRICK.

1. I know not the hour of his com-ing, Nor how he will speak to my heart;
2. I know not the bliss that awaits me, At rest with my Saviour a-bove;
3. Per-haps in the midst of my la-bor, A voice from the Lord I shall hear;
4. I know not, but oh, I am watching, My lamp ever burning and bright;

Or wheth-er at morning or mid-day, My spir-it to him will de-part.
I know not how soon I shall en-ter, And bathe in the o-cean of love.
Per-haps in the slumber of midnight, Its mes-sage may fall on my ear.
I know not if Je-sus will call me At morn-ing, at noon, or at night.

CHORUS.

But I know I shall wake in the likeness Of him I am longing to see;
I know   of him

I know that mine eyes shall behold him, And that is enough for me.
I know   is enough

Copyright, 1891, by Wm. J. Kirkpatrick. By per.

No. 158.

ON TO VICTORY !

Dedicated to Rev. B. C. Lippincott, D. D.

J. W. V.   J. W. Van De Venter.

1. There are foes that must be conquered, There are bat - tles we must win;
2. There are hosts of sin be - fore us, That ex - tend from sea to sea;
3. There are ma - ny dear ones dy - ing, They are fall - ing ev - ' ry-where;

There are lands that must be tak - en, That are go - ing down in sin,
There are ma - ny still in bond-age, There are slaves that must be free;
Let us brave - ly go and help them, They are lost and need our care;

Let us en - ter in the strug-gle, Ev - er march up-on our way,
Let us all be up and do - ing, Ev - er found with-in the fray,
Fall in line pre-pare for bat - tle, Let us fight as well as pray,

We must take the world for God and win the day.

CHORUS.

On...... to vic - to-ry ! on...... to vic - to-ry ! On...... to vic - to-ry ! the

foe must die !   On ..... to vic - to - ry we'll con-quer by and by.

No. 159. IS IT WELL WITH THY SOUL?

"Is it well with thee?"—2 Kings 4 : 26.

ANNIE L. JAMES.   W. D. HOWARD.

1. Tho' joys like the sun-shine il - lu - mine the way, And light- ly thy
2. Say, where is thy ref - uge for years that shall come? And what of thy
3. When storms of af - flic - tion a-round thee may fall, And bil- lows like
4. If he, thy Re - deem-er, is pre-cious to thee, And makes thee in

care may dis - pel,   Is Je - sus thy hope and thy an - chor to - day?
faith canst thou tell?   O where is thy treas-ure, thy heart and thy home?
mountains may roll,   O hast thou a trust that is great - er than all?
safe - ty to dwell, What-ev - er thy cares or temp-ta-tions may be,

CHORUS.

Is it well with thy soul, is it well?   Is it well...........
Is it well with thy soul, is it well?
Is it well with thy soul, is it well?
Praise the Lord! with thy soul is it well?

Is it well

rit.

With thy soul,........... Is it well, Is it well with thy soul?

With thy soul,

No. 160. JESUS WILL SAVE YOU NOW.

M. Louise Smith.   Howard E. Smith.

1. Brother, give heed to the Master's call, Je-sus will save you now,
2. What tho' your life has been stained by sin, Je-sus will save you now;
3. No one knows more of your pain than he, Je-sus will save you now;
4. Brother, de-fer not—this joy receive, Je-sus will save you now;

just now;

Come and confess—he'll forgive you all; Je-sus will save you now.
Just such as you can be cleansed by him, Je-sus will save you now.
See! now he pleads to give help so free, Je-sus will save you now.
New life you'll find if you but believe, Je-sus will save you now.

just now.

Chorus.

Yes, he will save! O yes, he will save! Je-sus will save you now;

just now;

It was for you that his life he gave, Je-sus will save you now.

just now.

No. 161.

I SHALL BE LIKE HIM.

W. A. S.

Rev. W. A. Spencer, D. D.

1. When I shall reach the more ex - cel-lent glo - ry, And all my
2. We shall not wait till the glo - ri - ous dawning Breaks on the
3. More and more like him, re - peat the blest sto - ry, O - ver and

tri- als are passed, I shall be- hold him, O won-der-ful sto- ry!
vis- ion so fair, Now we may welcome the heav- en- ly morning,
o - ver a - gain, Changed by his spir - it from glo - ry to glo - ry,

Chorus.

I shall be like him at last. }
Now we his im- age may bear. } I shall be like him, I shall be
I shall be sat - is - fied then. }

like him, And in his beau- ty shall shine; I shall be like him,

won- drous- ly like him, Je - sus, my Sav - iour di - vine.

No. 162. THE GOSPEL BELLS.

S. W. M.

S. Wesley Martin.

1. The Gos-pel bells are ring - ing O - ver land from sea to sea;
2. The Gos-pel bells in - vite us To a feast pre - pared for all;
3. The Gos-pel bells are joy - ful, As they ech - o far and wide,

Bless - ed news of free sal - va - tion Do they of - fer you and me.
Do not slight the in - vi - ta - tion, Nor re - ject the gra-cious call.
Bear - ing notes of per - fect par - don, Thro' a Sav - ior cru - ci - fied.

"For God so loved the world That His on - ly Son He gave,
"I am the bread of life; Eat of Me, thou hun - gry soul,
"Good ti-dings of great joy To all peo - ple I do bring,

Who - so - e'er be - liev - eth in Him Ev - er - last - ing life shall have."
Tho' your sins be red as crim - son, They shall be as white as wool."
Un - to you is born a Sav - ior, Which is Christ the Lord and King."

CHORUS.

Gos-pel bells, how they ring, O - ver land from sea to sea;
Gos-pel bells, how they ring,

THE GOSPEL BELLS.—Concluded.

Gospel bells　　　free-ly bring　　　Blessed news to you and me.
Gos-pel bells　　　free-ly bring!

No. 163.　　ONWARD, CHRISTIAN SOLDIERS!

SABINE BARING-GOULD.　　　　　　　　Tune, "Onward." 6, 5.

1. On-ward, Christian sol - diers! Marching as to war, With the cross of
2. Like a might-y ar - my Moves the Church of God; Brothers, we are
3. Crowns and thrones may perish, Kingdoms rise and wane, But the Church of
4. On - ward, then, ye peo-ple! Join our hap-py throng, Blend with ours your

Je - sus　Go - ing on be - fore; Christ, the roy - al Mas - ter,
tread-ing Where the saints have trod; We　are not di - vid - ed,
Je - sus　Con-stant will re - main; Gates of hell can nev - er
voi - ces　In the tri-umph song; Glo - ry, laud, and hon - or,

Leads a - gainst the foe; For-ward in - to bat - tle, See, His ban-ners go!
All one bod - y we; One in hope and doctrine, One in char - i - ty.
'Gainst that Church prevail; We have Christ's own promise, And that cannot fail.
Un - to Christ the King, This thro' countless a - ges Men and an-gels sing.

CHORUS.

Onward, Christian soldiers! Marching as to war, With the cross of Jesus Going on be - fore.

No. 164.   O JESUS, THOU ART STANDING.

WM. W. HOW.   (ST. HILDA. 7s, 6s. D.)   JUSTIN H. KNECHT, et. al.

1. O Je - sus, thou art standing   Out - side the fast-closed door,
2. O Je - sus, thou art knocking: And lo ! that hand is scarred,
3. O Je - sus, thou art pleading   In ac- cents meek and low,

In low - ly patience wait - ing   To pass the threshold o'er :
And thorns thy brow en - cir - cle,   And tears thy face have marred :
"I died for you, my chil - dren,   And will ye treat me   so?"

We bear the name of Chris - tians, His name and sign we bear :
Oh, love that pass- eth knowl- edge, So pa- tient - ly to wait !
O Lord, with shame and sor - row We o - pen now the door :

Oh, shame, thrice shame up-on   us ! To keep him stand- ing there.
Oh, sin that hath no e - qual, So fast to bar the gate !
Dear Sav- iour, en - ter, en - ter, And leave us nev - er - more !

No. 165. HE'LL NEVER FORSAKE HIS OWN.

C. H. G.

CHAS. H. GABRIEL.

1. While thro' this world of sin I go, I'll center my faith in Je-sus;
2. Tho' friends may fail and comforts flee, I'll center my faith in Je-sus;
3. For me he trod Gethsem-a-ne, I'll center my faith in Je-sus;
4. Tho' kindred ties of hope decay, I'll center my faith in Je-sus;
5. When in the solemn hour of death, I'll center my faith in Je-sus;
6. And when I reach my home on high, I'll center my faith in Je-sus;

I'll trust in him, for well I know, He'll never forsake his own.
His promise shall my comfort be, He'll never forsake his own.
For me he died on Cal-va-ry, He'll never forsake his own.
Tho' heav'n and earth should pass away, He'll never forsake his own.
And say with my ex-piring breath, He'll never forsake his own.
And sing while endless years go by, He'll never forsake his own.

CHORUS.

He'll never forsake his own,.... He'll never forsake his own;....
He'll never, no, never forsake his own,

With him I'll go, for well I know, He'll never forsake his own.

No. 166. THERE'S A WIDENESS.

FREDERICK W. FABER.　　　　　　　　LIZZIE S. TOURJEE.

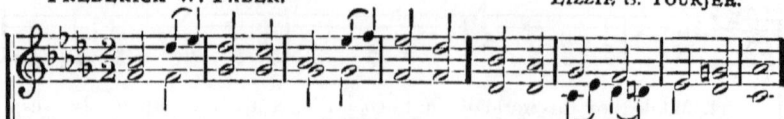

1. There's a wideness in God's mer-cy, Like the wideness of the sea:
2. There is welcome for the sin-ner, And more gra-ces for the good;
3. For the love of God is broad-er Than the meas-ure of man's mind;
4. If our love were but more sim-ple, We should take Him at His word;

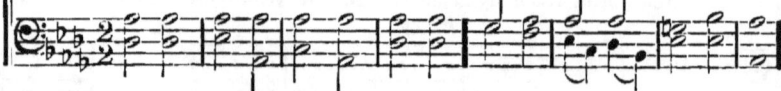

There's a kind-ness in His jus-tice, Which is more than lib-er-ty.
There is mer-cy with the Saviour; There is heal-ing in His blood.
And the heart of the E-ter-nal Is most won-der-ful-ly kind.
And our lives would be all sunshine In the sweetness of our Lord.

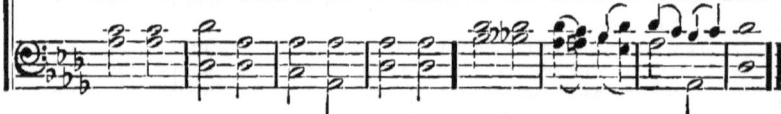

No. 167. HOLY GHOST, WITH LIGHT DIVINE.

LOUIS MOREAU GOTTSCHALK.

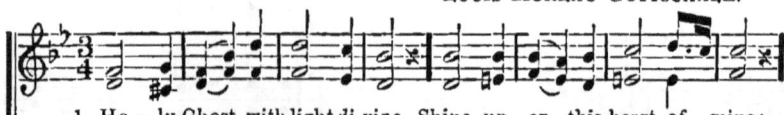

1. Ho-ly Ghost, with light di-vine, Shine up-on this heart of mine;
2. Ho-ly Ghost, with pow'r divine, Cleanse this guilt-y heart of mine;
3. Ho-ly Ghost, with joy di-vine, Cheer this saddened heart of mine;
4. Ho-ly Spir-it, all di-vine, Dwell with-in this heart of mine;

Chase the shades of night a-way, Turn my darkness in-to day.
Long hath sin, with-out con-trol, Held do-min-ion o'er my soul.
Bid my ma-ny woes de-part, Heal my wounded, bleeding heart.
Cast down ev-'ry i-dol-throne, Reign supreme—and reign a-lone.

No. 168. LOYALTY TO THE MASTER.

E. E. Hewitt.   Wm. J. Kirkpatrick.

1. Loy-al-ty to the Mas-ter, loy-al-ty to the King; Loy-al-ty now and
2. Loy-al-ty to the Mas-ter; letting him lead the way; Glo-ri-ous is his
3. Loy-al-ty to the Mas-ter; looking to him a-lone, Turning a-way from

ev - er, cheer-i - ly let us sing; Wholly at his command - ment,
ban - ner, fol-low it ev - 'ry day; In - to the 'midst of bat - tle,
e - vil, Je-sus will keep his own; Onward, still on-ward press - ing,

let ev-'ry soldier be, Joyful-ly serving Je-sus, serving with loy-al-ty.
conquering as we go, Vic-to-ry he has promised o-ver the dead-ly foe.
seeing the star-ry prize Waiting for all the faithful, meeting beyond the skies.

CHORUS.

Loy - al sol-diers, let us joy-ful-ly march a-long, For - - ward,
Joy-ful-ly march,

for - - ward, with a triumphant song; On - ward, on - ward, a
stead-i-ly march,   Joy-ful-ly march, stead-i-ly march,

happy and loy-al throng, Loy-al to our Saviour and our King............
to our Saviour and our King.

No. 169. SOME DAY I AM GOING THERE.

C. H. M.

Mrs. C. H. Morris.

1. I have heard of a beauti-ful cit - y, A city where cometh no night,
2. A city where death never en - ters, Nor sickness, nor sorrow, nor pain,
3. Some day the great King in his beau-ty, My wondering eyes shall be-hold,

Tho' a ray from the sun never shin-eth, For Je-sus the Lamb is the light;
And ties which on earth have been broken Shall be re-u-nit-ed a - gain;
Some day and my feet shall be treading Those beautiful pavements of gold;

I have heard how its walls are of jasper, How the streets are all golden and fair;
No mansion on earth I am shar-ing, My heart and my treasure are there;
Not worthy the least of his no-tice, Not worthy one moment of care;

A home for the blood-wash'd and ransom'd, And some day I'm go-ing there.
And Je-sus my place is pre-par-ing, And some day I'm go-ing there.
But Je-sus has bid-den me wel-come, And some day I'm go-ing there.

CHORUS.

Some day, some day I am go - ing To that home so bright and fair;

With my heart with love o'er-flow - ing, Some day I am go-ing there.

EVERY WORD I BELIEVE.

Rev. Johnson Oatman, Jr.   Wm. J. Kirkpatrick.

Moderato.

1. If you ask me why I'm hap-py as I jour-ney down life's road,
2. We are not al-lowed to wan-der thro' this world with-out a Guide,
3. He in-forms us for our com-fort that thro' life he'll be our Friend,
4. He has told us of a cit-y where the streets are paved with gold,

Why it is I do not car-ry on the way a heav-y load,
For, to keep our feet from stray-ing his own word has been ap-plied,
That if we will on-ly trust him he'll go with us to the end,
Where the faithful shall be gath-ered and their Saviour's face be-hold,

It's because my Sav-iour tells me that my bur-den he'll re-ceive,
And we read there that the sentence of a sin-ner he'll re-prieve,
That his Spir-it will be with us while we do not slight nor grieve,
He has promised at its por-tals that our souls he will re-ceive,

CHORUS.

And I believe it, ev-'ry word I believe. I believe it, ev'ry
And I

I be-lieve.....

word I believe, I receive it, ev'ry word I receive; Je-sus tells me my

I re-ceive...

wants he will relieve, And I believe it, ev-'ry word I believe.
And I

PASS ME NOT.

FANNY J. CROSBY.

W. H. DOANE.

1. Pass me not, O gen-tle Sav-iour, Hear my hum-ble cry; While on
2. Let me at a throne of mer-cy Find a sweet re-lief; Kneel-ing
3. Trust-ing on-ly in Thy mer-it, Would I seek Thy face; Heal my
4. Thou the Spring of all my com-fort, More than life to me, Whom have

oth-ers Thou art smil-ing, Do not pass me by.
there in deep con-tri-tion, Help my un-be-lief.
wounded, bro-ken spir-it, Save me by Thy grace. } Sav-iour, Sav-iour,
I on earth beside Thee? Whom in heav'n but Thee?

CHORUS.

Hear my humble cry, While on others Thou art calling, Do not pass me by.

Copyright, 1870, by W. H. Doane. Used by permission.

MAKE ME A BLESSING TO-DAY.

Rev. H. J. ZELLEY.

H. L. GILMOUR.

1. I do not ask to choose my path, Lord, lead me in Thy way;
2. A-round me, Lord, are sin-ful men, Who scorn and dis-o-bey;
3. To those who once Thy love have known, But now are far a-stray;
4. Some saints of Thine are in dis-tress, And for de-liverance pray;
5. What-ev-er er-rand Thou hast, Lord, Send me, and I'll o-bey;

Inspire each tho't and prompt each word, And make me a bless-ing to-day.
Use me to win them from their sins, And make me a bless-ing to-day.
Help me to lead them back to Thee, And make me a bless-ing to-day.
O let me go and help them Lord, And make me a bless-ing to-day.
Use me in an-y way Thou wilt, And make me a bless-ing to-day.

Copyright, 1894, by H. L. Gilmour.

CHORUS.

Bless me, Lord, and make me a blessing, I'll glad-ly Thy message con-vey;

Use me to help some poor, needy soul, And make me a blessing to - day.

No. 173 THOUGH YOUR SINS BE AS SCARLET.

FANNY J. CROSBY.   W. H. DOANE.

DUET. *Gently.*

1. "Tho' your sins be as scar - let, They shall be as white as snow; as snow;
2. Hear the voice that entreats you, O re - turn ye un - to God! to God!
3. He'll for-give your transgressions, And remember them no more; no more;

QUARTET.

Tho' they be red...................... like crim-son, They shall be as wool;"
He is of great...................... com-pas- sion, And of wondrous love;
"Look un - to me,...................... ye peo - ple," Saith the Lord your God;

Tho' they be red

DUET. *p*   QUARTET. *f*

"Tho' your sins be as scar - let, Tho' your sins be as scar - let,
Hear the voice that en - treats you, Hear the voice that en-treats you,
He'll for - give your trans-gres-sions, He'll for - give your transgressions,

p ritard.

They shall be as white as snow, They shall be at white as snow."
O re - turn ye un - to God! O re - turn ye un - to God!
And re - mem - ber them no more, And re - mem-ber them no more.

No. 174. ALMOST PERSUADED.

P. P. Bliss.   P. P. Bliss.

1. "Al-most per-suad-ed," Now to be-lieve; "Al-most per-suad-ed,"
2. "Al-most per-suad-ed," Come, come to-day; "Al-most per-suad-ed,"
3. "Al-most per-suad-ed," Har-vest is past! "Al-most per-suad-ed,"

Christ to re-ceive; Seems now some soul to say, "Go, Spir-it,
Turn not a-way; Je-sus in-vites you here, An-gels are
Doom comes at last! "Al-most" can not a-vail; "Al-most" is

go thy way, Some more con-ven-ient day On thee I'll call."
lingering near, Pray'rs rise from hearts so dear: O wan-d'rer come.
but to fail! Sad, sad, that bit-ter wail— "Al-most—but lost!"

No. 175. RESCUE THE PERISHING.

F. J. Crosby.   W. H. Doane.

1. Res-cue the per-ish-ing, Care for the dy-ing, Snatch them in pit-y from
2 Tho' they are slighting Him, Still He is wait-ing, Wait-ing the pen-i-tent
3. Down in the human heart, Crush'd by the tempter, Feel-ings lie bur-ied that
4. Res-cue the per-ish-ing, Du-ty demands it; Strength for thy la-bor the

sin and the grave; Weep o'er the err-ing one, Lift up the fal-len,
child to re-ceive. Plead with them earnest-ly, Plead with them gent-ly;
grace can re-store; Touched by a lov-ing heart, Wak-ened by kind-ness,
Lord will pro-vide: Back to the nar-row way Pa-tient-ly win them;

RESCUE THE PERISHING.—Concluded.

CHORUS.

Tell them of Je - sus the might - y to save.
He will for - give if they on - ly be - lieve.
Chords that were bro - ken will vi - brate once more.
Tell the poor wand'rer a Sav - iour has died.

Res - cue the per - ish - ing,

Care for the dy - ing; Je - sus is mer - ci - ful, Je - sus will save.

No. 176.   SAFE IN THE ARMS OF JESUS.

FANNY J. CROSBY.   W. H. DOANE.

1. Safe in the arms of Je - sus, Safe on His gen - tle breast—
2. Safe in the arms of Je - sus, Safe from cor - rod - ing care;
3. Je - sus, my heart's dear ref - uge, Je - sus has died for me;

There by His love o'er - shad - ed, Sweet-ly my soul shall rest.
Safe from the world's temp-ta - tions, Sin can not harm me there.
Firm on the Rock of A - ges, Ev - er my trust shall be.

Hark! 'tis the voice of an - gels, Borne in a song to me,
Free from the blight of sor - row, Free from my doubts and fears;
Here let me wait with pa - tience, Wait till the night is o'er;

D. C. Chorus first four lines.

O - ver the fields of glo - ry, O - ver the jas - per sea.
On - ly a few more tri - als, On - ly a few more tears.
Wait till I see the morn - ing, Break on the gold - en shore.

No. 177. I SHALL BE NO STRANGER THERE.

E. E. HEWITT. A. F. BOURNE.

1. When the pearl - y gates are o - pened To a sin-ner " sav'd by grace,"
2. Thro' time's ev - er-changing sea - sons, I am pressing t' ward the goal;
3. There my dear Re-deem-er liv - eth, Bless-ed Lamb up - on the throne;

When thro' ev - er-last-ing mer - cy, I be-hold my Saviour's face,
'Tis my heart's sweet na-tive coun-try, 'Tis the home-land of my soul;
By the crim-son marks up-on them, He will sure - ly claim His own.

When I en - ter in the man-sions Of the cit - y bright and fair,
Ma - ny lov'd ones, cloth'd with beauty, In those wondrous glo - ries share;
So, when-ev - er sad or lone - ly, Look be-yond the earth-ly care;

I shall have a roy - al wel-come, For I'll be no stranger there.
When I rise, redeemed, for - giv - en, I shall be no stranger there.
Wea - ry child of God, re-mem - ber, You will be no stranger there.

CHORUS.

I shall be no stranger there, Je-sus will my place pre-pare;
I shall be no stran - ger there, Je - sus will my place pre - pare;

He will meet me, He will greet me, I shall be no stranger there.
He will meet me, He will greet me, I shall be

No. 178. ALL IN THY HANDS.

IDA L. REED.   J. LINCOLN HALL.

DUETT FOR SOPRANO AND TENOR OR ALTO.

1. All in Thy hands I leave, dear Lord, All of life's dai-ly fret and sting, All of my griefs what-
2. All in Thy hands each hour, each day, Whether cares may be great or small, Jesus, dear Lord, I
3. All in Thy hands my Lord and King, All of life's sorrow, toil and pain, All of my cares I
4. All in Thy hands O rich reward, Peace and joy it doth bring to me, Dai-ly I rest in

CHORUS.

e'er they are, This to my soul sweet peace doth bring,
lean on Thee, Thou art my ref-uge and my all,
bring to Thee, Thy love my soul will e'er sus-tain,
Thee, dear Lord, Dai-ly I'm lean-ing more on Thee.

All in Thy hands like a glad refrain,

Cometh the promise so sweet, "Bring me Thy burden, I will sustain, Give to Thee strength complete." complete."

No. 179. LORD, I'M COMING HOME.

W. J. K.   W. J. KIRKPATRICK.

With great feeling.

1. I've wandered far a-way from God, Now I'm coming home; The paths of sin too long I've trod,
2. I've wasted ma-ny precious years, Now I'm coming home; I now repent with bitter tears,
3. I've tired of sin and straying, Lord, Now I'm coming home; I'll trust Thy love, believe Thy word,
4. My soul is sick, my heart is sore, Now I'm coming home; My strength renew, my hope restore,

D. S.—Open wide Thine arms of love.

FINE. CHORUS.   D. S.

Lord, I'm coming home. Coming home, coming home, Nev-er more to roam;

Lord, I'm coming home.

5 My only hope, my only plea,
   Now I'm coming home,
That Jesus died, and died for me,
   Lord, I'm coming home.

6 I need His cleansing blood I know,
   Now I'm coming home;
O, wash me whiter than the snow,
   Lord, I'm coming home.

No. 180. WHEN THE ROLL IS CALLED UP YONDER.

J. M. B.   J. M. BLACK.

1. When the trum-pet of the Lord shall sound, and time shall be no more,
2. On that bright and cloudless morning, when the dead in Christ shall rise,
3. Let us la - bor for the Mas-ter from the dawn till set-ting sun,

And the morning breaks, eternal, bright and fair; When the saved of earth shall
And the glo - ry of His res - ur-rec-tion share; When His chosen ones shall
Let us talk of all His wondrous love and care, Then, when all of life is

gath - er o - ver on the oth - er shore, And the roll is called up
gath - er to their home be-yond the skies, And the roll is called up
o - ver, and our work on earth is done, And the roll is called up

CHORUS.

yon-der, I'll be there. When the roll........ is called up yon - - der,
When the roll is called up yon-der, I'll be there,

When the roll.............. is called up yon - - der, When the
When the roll is called up yon-der, I'll be there,

roll......... is called up yon-der, When the roll is called up yonder, I'll be there.
When the roll

No. 181.   THE HOMELAND.

Rev. H. R. HAWEIS.   ARTHUR S. SULLIVAN.

1. The Homeland! the Homeland! The land of the free-born, There's no night in the
2. My Lord is in the Homeland, With angels bright and fair,—There's no sin in the

Homeland, But aye the fadeless morn; I'm sighing for the Homeland, My heart is
Homeland, And no tempta-tion there; The voic-es of the Homeland Are ring-ing

ach-ing here, There's no pain in the Homeland, To which I'm drawing near.
in my ears, And when I think of the Homeland, My eyes gush out with tears.

3. For those I love in the Homeland Are calling me a-way, To the rest and peace of the

Homeland, And the life beyond de-cay. For there's no death in the Homeland, There's no

sor-row a-bove: Christ, bring us all to the Homeland Of His e-ter-nal love.

No. 182. SAVE THE FALLEN.

Mrs. Loula K. Rogers.

W. G. Aleshine.

1. Save the fall-en, save the fall-en, Canst thou care-less pass them by;
2. Raise the fall-en, raise the fall-en, Snatch them quickly from the grave,
3. Save the fall-en, save the fall-en, Clouds are gath'ring o'er the sky;
4. Lift the fall-en, lift the fall-en, In their hearts lie bur-ied deep;

Wilt thou leave thine erring neighbor, Leave him all a-lone to die?
Tell them Je-sus will for-give them, That he died their souls to save.
He will per-ish in the dark-ness, Leave, oh, leave him not to die!
Feel-ings that the touch of kind-ness, May a-wake from deathly sleep.

Then, O Chris-tian speak the mes-sage, Speak it, speak it while you may;
Gen-tly breathe his name so pre-cious, Humbly call-ing ere too late;
Let thy mer-cy beam dear Sav-iour, O'er the poor be-night-ed soul;
Of his love, O Christians tell them,—Christ hast promised un-to all—

Love thy neighbor as thy-self, Pass him not an-oth-er day.
It hath pow'r to sweep a-way, All the tempt-er's cru-el hate.
Draw the wand'rer close to thee, Keep him ev-er in the fold.
And the par-don full and free, Of-fered un-to those who fall.

CHORUS.

Save, O Chris-tian, save the fall-en, Je-sus bids you bring them in;

Save, O Christian,   Je-sus bids you

From the hedg-es and the highways, Save their souls from death and sin.

From the hedges   Save their souls

No. 183. VOLUNTEERS, TO THE FRONT!

Mrs. E. E. WILLIAMS.   M. PAULINE GILMOUR.

Martial style.

1. Vol - un - teers are want- ed! hear the stir- ring call,   O be swift to
2. Vol - un - teers are want- ed! val - iant men and true,   In the ranks, my
3. Vol - un - teers are want- ed! for on land and sea   Satan's starving
4. Vol - un - teers are want- ed! on the bat - tle-plain   Soldiers brave are
5. Vol - un - teers are want- ed! let the ranks be filled,   Soon the din of

an - swer, comrades, one and all; Gird - ing on your ar - mor,
broth - er, there is room for you; Christ is the Command - er,
bond - men clam - or to be free; Hast - en to their res - cue,
fall - ing, ne'er to fight a - gain; Who will take their plac - es
bat - tle will in peace be stilled; See! the clouds are lift - ing,

haste to march a - way, For the Lord is calling, "to the front to - day!"
let us all o - bey, When he gives the or - der, "to the front to - day!"
if you still delay Blood - bought souls must perish, to the front to - day!
in the dead- ly fray? Who will march with Jesus to the front to - day?
soon they'll clear away, Glo - ry gilds the heights along the front to - day.

CHORUS.

A - way to the bat - tle-field, a - way, a - way! The King calls for
A - way, a - way to the bat - tle-field, a - way,

sol - diers in his ranks to - day; Hear the bu - gle call - ing,
sol - diers in his ranks to - day;

in - to line be fall- ing, Forth to the bat- tle-field, a - way, a - way!

No. 184. DEPTH OF MERCY.

CHARLES WESLEY. From STEVENSON.

1. { Depth of mer-cy! can there be / Mer-cy still re-served for me? }
   { Can my God His wrath for-bear? / Me, the chief of sin-ners spare? }
2. { I have long with-stood His grace, / Long provoked Him to His face: }
   { Would not hearken to His calls; / Grieved Him by a thousand falls. }
3. { Now in-cline me to re-pent; / Let me now my sins la-ment; }
   { Now my foul re-volt de-plore, / Weep, be-lieve, and sin no more. }

CHORUS.

God is love! I know, I feel; Je-sus lives, and loves me still;

Je - - sus lives, He lives and loves me still.

No. 185. PERFECT PEACE.

FRANCES R. HAVERGAL. J. MOUNTAIN.

Joyful.

1. Like a riv-er, glo-rious Is God's per-fect peace, O-ver all vic-
2. Hid-den in the hol-low Of His bless-ed hand, Nev-er foe can
3. Ev-'ry joy or tri-al Fall-eth from a-bove, Traced up-on our

to - rious In its bright in-crease; Per-fect, yet it flow-eth
fol - low, Nev-er trait-or stand; Not a surge of wor-ry,
di - al By the Sun of Love. We may trust Him ful-ly

Cho.—Stayed up-on Je-ho-vah,

Chorus D.S.

Full-er ev-'ry day,— Per-fect, yet it grow-eth Deep-er all the way.
Not a shade of care, Not a blast of hur-ry Touch the spir-it there.
All for us to do; They who trust Him wholly Find Him whol-ly true.

Hearts are ful-ly blest; Finding, as He prom-ised, Per-fect peace and rest.

JESUS SAVES ME NOW.

Old Melody.

Joyful.

1. { Je - sus hath died and hath ris - en a - gain, Par-don and peace to be - stow; }
   { Ful - ly I trust Him; from sin's guilt-y stain, Je - sus saves me now. }
2. { Sin's con-dem-na-tion is o - ver and gone, Je - sus a - lone knoweth how; }
   { Life and Sal - va-tion my soul hath put on: Je - sus saves me now. }
3. { Sa - tan may tempt, but he nev - er shall reign, *That* Christ will never al - low; }
   { Doubts I have bur - ied, and this is my strain, "Je - sus saves me new." }

CHORUS.

Je - sus saves me now; Je - sus saves me now; Yes, Je - sus saves me

all the time; Je-sus saves me now.

4 Resting in Jesus, abiding in Him,
  Gladly my faith can avow,—
  Never again need my pathway be dim
  Jesus saves me now.

5 Jesus is stronger than Satan and sin,
  Satan to Jesus must bow;
  Therefore I triumph without and within
  Jesus saves me now.

6 Sorrow and pain may beset me about,
  Nothing can darken my brow;
  Battling in faith, I can joyfully shout;
  "Jesus saves me now."

No. 187. ALL HAIL THE POWER.

EDWARD PERRONET. WILLIAM SHRUBSOLE.

1. All hail the pow'r of Je-sus' Name! Let an-gels prostrate fall, Bring forth the roy-al
2. Crown Him, ye morning stars of light, Who fixed this floating ball; Now hail the strength of
3. Crown Him, ye martyrs of your God Who from His al - tar call; Ex - tol the Stem of

di - a - dem, And crown Him, crown Him, crown Him, Crown Him Lord of all.
Israel's might, And crown Him, crown Him, crown Him, Crown Him Lord of all.
Jes - se's rod, And crown Him, crown Him, crown Him, Crown Him Lord of all.

4 Ye seed of Israel's chosen race,
  Ye ransomed of the fall;
  Hail Him who saves you by His grace,
  And crown Him Lord of all.

5 Sinners, whose love can ne'er forget
  The wormwood and the gall,
  Go, spread your trophies at His feet,
  And crown Him Lord of all.

6 Let every kindred, every tribe,
  On this terrestrial ball,
  To Him all majesty ascribe,
  And crown Him Lord of all.

7 O that with yonder sacred throng
  We at His feet may fall!
  We'll join the everlasting song,
  And crown Him Lord of all.

No. 188. WHAT ARE YOU DOING FOR JESUS?

EMILY P. MILLER.　　　　　　　　　　　J. LINCOLN HALL.

1. What are you do-ing for Je-sus, As you jour-ney thro' life?
2. What are you do-ing for Je-sus? Are you striv-ing each day,
3. What are you do-ing for Je-sus As the days go by?
4. What are you do-ing for Je-sus? Soon comes set-ting of sun;

Sow-ing the grain for the har-vest, Or scat-ter-ing seeds of strife?
By lit-tle acts of kind-ness, To bright-en some one's way?
Tell-ing the lone and the wea-ry, Of rest be-yond the sky?
Hast-en and tell the glad tid-ings, Lest you leave some work un-done.

CHORUS.
What are you do - - ing, Do - - ing for Je - sus?
What are you do-ing for Je-sus your friend? What are you doing for Jesus to-day?

What are you do - - ing, As the days go by?...............
What are you do-ing for Je-sus your friend, As the days go by, days go by?

What are you do - - ing? Do - - ing, for Je - sus?
What are you do-ing for Je-sus your friend? What are you doing for Jesus to-day?

What are you do - - ing As the days go by?...............
What are you do-ing for Je-sus your friend, As the days go by, days go by?

No. 189. I WILL SHOUT HIS PRAISE IN GLORY.

P. H. DINGMAN.

JNO. R. SWENEY.

1. You ask what makes me happy, my heart so free from care, It is because my
2. I was a friendless wand'rer till Je-sus took me in, My life was full of
3. I wish that ev'ry sinner before his throne would bow; He waits to bid them
4. I mean to live for Jesus while here on earth I stay, And when his voice shall

Sav-iour in mer-cy heard my pray'r; He brought me out of dark-ness and
sor - row, my heart was full of sin; But when the blood so pre-cious spoke
welcome, he longs to bless them now; If they but knew the rap - ture that
call me to realms of end-less day; As one by one we gath - er, re-

now the light I see; O blessed, loving Saviour! to him the praise shall be.
par-don to my soul; O blissful, blissful moment! 'twas joy beyond control.
in his love I see, They'd come and shout salvation, and sing his praise with me.
joic-ing on the shore, We'll shout his praise in glo-ry, and sing for ev-ermore.

CHORUS.

I will shout his praise in glo - ry,.................... And we'll
So will I, so will I,

all sing hal-le - lu-jah in heav-en by and by; I will shout his praise in

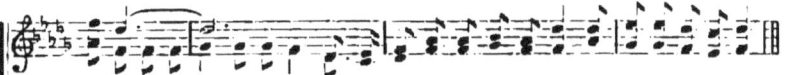

glo-ry,............ And we'll all sing halle-lu-jah in heaven by and by.
So will I, so will I,

SAVED TO THE UTTERMOST.

W. J. K.

WM. J. KIRKPATRICK.

1. Saved to the ut - ter-most: I am the Lord's; Je - sus, my
2. Saved to the ut - ter-most: Je - sus is near; Keep - ing me
3. Saved to the ut - ter-most: this I can say, "Once all was
4. Saved to the ut - ter-most: cheer - ful - ly sing Loud hal - le -

Sav - iour, sal - va - tion af - fords; Gives me His Spir - it a
safe - ly, He cast - eth out fear; Trust - ing His prom - is - es,
dark - ness, but now it is day; Beau - ti - ful vis - ions of
lu - ias to Je - sus, my King! Ran-somed and par - doned, re -

wit - ness with - in, Whisp'ring of par - don, and sav - ing from sin.
how I am blest; Lean - ing up - on Him, how sweet is my rest.
glo - ry I see, Je - sus in bright-ness re - vealed un - to me.
deemed by His blood, Cleans'd from un - right-eous-ness, glo - ry to God.

REFRAIN.

Saved, saved, saved to the ut - termost: Saved, saved, by pow - er di - vine:

Saved, saved, saved to the ut - ter-most: Je - sus, the Sav-iour, is mine.

Copyright, 1875, by Wm. J. Kirkpatrick.

THE COMFORTER HAS COME!

Rev. F. BOTTOME, D. D.

WM. J. KIRKPATRICK.

1. Oh, spread the ti - dings round, wher - ev - er man is found Wher -
2. The long, long night is past, the morn - ing breaks at last; And
3. Lo, the great King of kings, with heal - ing in His wings, To
4. O bound-less Love di - vine! how shall this tongue of mine To
5. Sing, till the ech - oes fly a - bove the vault-ed sky, And

Copyright, 1890, by W. J. Kirkpatrick.

THE COMFORTER HAS COME!—Concluded.

ev - er hu - man hearts and hu - man woes a - bound; Let ev - 'ry Christian
hushed the dreadful wail and fu - ry of the blast, As o'er the gold - en
ev - 'ry cap - tive soul a full de - liv'rance brings; And thro' the va - cant
wond'ring mor - tals tell the matchless grace di - vine—That I, a child of
all the saints a - bove to all be - low re - ply, In strains of end - less

D.S.—Ho - ly Ghost from heav'n, The Fa - ther's promise giv'n; Oh, spread the ti - dings

FINE.

tongue pro - claim the joy - ful sound: The Com - fort - er has come!
hills the day ad - vanc - es fast! The Com - fort - er has come!
cells the song of tri - umph rings: The Com - fort - er has come!
hell, should in His im - age shine! The Com - fort - er has come!
love, the song that ne'er will die: The Com - fort - er has come!

round, Wher - ev - er man is found—The Com - fort - er has come!

CHORUS.   D.S.

The Com - fort - er has come, The Com - fort - er has come! The

No. 192.   HOLY SPIRIT, FAITHFUL GUIDE.

M. M. W.   M. M. WELLS

FINE.

1. { Ho - ly Spir - it, faith - ful Guide, Ev - er near the Christian's side, }
   { Gen - tly lead us by the hand, Pil - grims in a des - ert land; }

D.C.—Whisp'ring soft - ly, wand'rer, come! Fol - low me, I'll guide thee home.

D. C.

Wea - ry souls for - e'er re - joice, While they hear that sweet - est voice,

2 Ever present, truest Friend,
Ever near, Thine aid to lend,
Leave us not to doubt and fear,
Groping on in darkness drear.
When the storms are raging sore,
Hearts grow faint, and hopes give o'er;
Whisper softly, wand'rer come!
Follow me, I'll guide thee home.

3 When our days of toil shall cease,
Waiting still for sweet release,
Nothing left but heaven and prayer,
Wond'ring if our names are there;
Wading deep the dismal flood,
Pleading naught but Jesus' blood,
Whisper softly, wand'rer, come!
Follow me, I'll guide thee home.

No. 193. MY FAITH LOOKS UP TO THEE.

RAY PALMER. (OLIVET. 6s, 4s.) LOWELL MASON.

1. My faith looks up to Thee,Thou Lamb of Cal-va-ry, Sav-iour di-vine; Now hear me
2. May Thy rich grace impart Strength to my fainting heart, My zeal inspire! As Thou hast

while I pray. Take all my guilt a-way, O let me from this day Be whol-ly thine!
died for me, O may my love to Thee Pure,warm, and changeless be, A living fire!

3 While life's dark maze I tread,
  And griefs around me spread,
    Be Thou my Guide;
  Bid darkness turn to day,
  Wipe sorrow's tears away,
  Nor let me ever stray
    From Thee aside.

4 When ends life's transient dream,
  When death's cold. sullen stream
    Shall o'er me roll;
  Blest Saviour, then, in love,
  Fear and distrust remove;
  O bear me safe above,
    A ransomed soul!

No. 194. MY COUNTRY! 'TIS OF THEE.

S. F. SMITH. (AMERICA. 6s, 4s.) Ad. HENRY CAREY.

1. My country! 'tis of thee, Sweet land of lib-er-ty. Of thee I sing: Land where my
2. My na-tive country. thee, Land of the no-ble. free. Thy name I love; I love thy
3. Let music swell the breeze, And ring from all the trees Sweet freedom's song; Let mortal
4. Our Father's God, to Thee, Au-thor of lib-er-ty. To Thee we sing; Long may our

cres.

father's died! Land of the Pilgrim's pride! From ev'ry mountain side. Let freedom ring.
rocks and rills, Thy woods and templed hills; My heart with rapture thrills, Like that above.
tongues awake, Let all that breathe partake, Let rocks their silence break, The sound prolong.
land be bright With freedom's holy light; Pro-tect us by Thy might,Great God, our King!

No. 195. COME, THOU ALMIGHTY KING.

C. WESLEY. (ITALIAN HYMN. 6s, 4.) FELICE GIARDINI.

1. Come,Thou al-might-y King. Help us Thy name to sing, Help us to praise; Father all-
2. Come,Thou incarnate Word, Gird on Thy mighty sword,Our pray'r attend ; Come and Thy
3. Come, ho-ly Com-fort-er, Thy sacred wit-ness bear In this glad hour; Thou who al-
4. To the great One and Three E-ter-nal prais-es be Hence—evermore! His sov'reign

COME, THOU ALMIGHTY KING. Concluded.

glo - ri-ous, O'er all vic - to - ri-ous, Come, and reign o - ver us. Ancient of Days.
people bless, And give Thy word success: Spir-it of ho - li-ness, On us de-scend!
might-y art, Now rule in ev-'ry heart, And ne'er from us depart, Spir-it of pow'r!
maj-es-ty May we in glo-ry see. And to e-ter-ni-ty Love and a - dore.

No. 196. **HAPPY DAY.**

P. DODDRIDGE. E. F. RIMBAULT.

1. { O hap-py day, that fixed my choice On Thee, my Saviour and my God!
   { Well may this glowing heart re-joice, And tell its raptures all a-broad. } Hap-py

FINE. D.S.

day, happy day, When Jesus wash'd my sins away! { He taught me how to watch and pray,
                                                  { And live re-joicing ev-'ry day. }

2 O happy bond, that seals my vows
To Him who merits all my love!
Let cheerful anthems fill His house,
While to that sacred shrine I move.

3 'Tis done: the great transaction's done!
I am my Lord's and He is mine;
He drew me, and I followed on.
Charmed to confess the voice divine.

No. 197. **REVIVE US AGAIN.**

WM. P. MACKAY. J. J. HUSBAND.

1. We praise Thee, O God! for the Son of Thy love, For Jesus who died, and is now gone above.

CHORUS.

Hal-le-lu-jah! thine the glo-ry, Hal-le-lu-jah! A-men, Re-vive us a-gain.

2 We praise Thee, O God! for Thy Spirit of light,
Who has shown us our Saviour, and scattered our night.

3 All glory and praise to the Lamb that was slain,
Who has borne all our sins, and has cleansed every stain.

4 All glory and praise to the God of all grace,
Who has bought us, and sought us, and guided our way.

5 Revive us again; fill each heart with Thy love;
May each soul be rekindled with fire from above.

No. 198.   TAKE MY LIFE AND LET IT BE.   Handel.

(music)

1. Take my life and let it be Con-se-crated, Lord, to thee; Take my hands and
2. Take my feet and let them be Swift and beauti- ful for thee; Take my voice and
3. Take my lips and let them be Filled with messages from thee; Take my sil - ver
4. Take my moments and my days, Let them flow in endless praise; Take my in-tel -

(music)

let them move At the impulse of thy love, At the im-pulse of thy love.
let me sing, Always, on- ly for my King, Always on - ly for my King.
and my gold, Not a mite would I withhold, Not a mite would I with-hold.
lect and use Ev'ry pow'r as thou shalt choose, Ev'ry pow'r as thou shalt choose.

5 Take my will and make it thine,
  It shall be no longer mine :
Take my heart, it is thine own,
  It shall be thy royal throne.

6 Take my love, my God, I pour
  At thy feet its treasure store,
Take myself, and I will be
  Ever, only, all for thee.

No. 199.   LOST, BUT NOT FORSAKEN.
J. W. V.   J. W. Van DeVenter.

(music)

1. Tho' a sin- ner, sick and dy- ing, Je-sus nev - er left my heart; I could always
2. Tho' I oft- en spurn'd his pleading, Still he plead without the door; Till at last I
3. O the joy that filled my be- ing! It was glo - ry in my soul! When I bid the

CHORUS.

hear his knocking 'Till he bade my sins depart. }
swung it o- pen, Open wide, to close no more. } I was lost, but not forsaken, I was
Saviour enter, And his power made me whole. }

ruin - ed by my sin; But the Lord continued knocking 'Till at last I let him in.

Copyright, 1899, by Hall-Mack Co.

No. 200.   SUN OF MY SOUL.
John Keble.   HURSLEY. L. M.   Arr. by Henry Monk.

(music)

1. Sun of my soul, thou Sav-iour dear, It is not night if thou be near;
2. When the soft dews of kind-ly sleep My wearied eye - lids gen- tly sleep,
3. Abide with me from morn till eve, For without thee I can- not live;
4. If some poor wand'ring child of thine Have spurn'd to-day, the voice divine,

SUN OF MY SOUL.—Concluded.

O may no earth-born cloud a - rise To hide thee from thy ser-vant's eyes.
Be my last thou't, how sweet to rest For-ev - er on my Saviour's breast.
A- bide with me when night is nigh, For without thee I dare not die.
Now, Lord, the gracious work be - gin; Let him no more lie down in sin.

No. 201.   O, NOW I SEE THE CRIMSON WAVE.

PHŒBE PALMER.   MRS. JOSEPH F. KNAPP.

1. O, now I see the crim-son wave, The fountain deep and wide, Je -
2. I rise to walk in heav'n's own light, A -bove the world and sin, With
3. A - mazing grace! 'tis heav'n be-low, To feel the blood ap - plied; And

sus, my Lord, mighty to save, Points to his wounded side. } The cleansing stream I
heart made pure, and garments white, And Christ enthron'd within. } O praise the Lord, it
Je - sus, on - ly Je-sus know, My Je-sus cru - ci - fied.

REFRAIN.

see, I see, I plunge, and O, it cleanseth me!
cleanseth me, It (*Omit*.............................) cleanseth me, yes, cleanseth me !

No. 202.   JUST AS I AM.

CHARLOTTE ELLIOT.   WOODWORTH. L. M.   WM. BRADBURY.

1. Just as I am! with-out one plea, But that thy blood was shed for me,
2. Just as I am! and wait-ing not, To rid my soul of one dark blot;
3. Just as I am! tho' tossed a- bout, With many a con-flict, many a doubt,
4. Just as I am! poor, wretched, blind, Sight, riches, heal-ing of the mind,
5. Just as I am! thou wilt re-ceive, Wilt welcome, pardon, cleanse, relieve,

And that thou bid'st me come to thee, O Lamb of God! I come, I come!
To thee, whose blood can cleanse each spot, O Lamb of God! I come, I come!
Fightings and fears within, with-out, O Lamb of God! I come, I come!
Yea, all I need, in thee to find, O Lamb of God! I come, I come!
Be-cause thy promise I be-lieve; O Lamb of God! I come, I come!

No. 203. HEAVEN IS MY HOME.

THOS. R. TAYLOR.

Scotch Air.

1. I'm but a stran-ger here, Heaven is my home; Earth is a
2. What though the tem-pest rage, Heaven is my home; Short is my
3. There at my Sav-iour's side, Heaven is my home; I shall be

des-ert drear, Heaven is my home. Danger and sorrow stand, Round me on
pil-grimage, Heaven is my home. Time's cold and wintry blast. Soon will be
glo-ri-fied, Heaven is my home. There are the good and blest, Those I loved

ev-'ry hand, Heav'n is my fa-ther-land, Heav'n is my home.
o-ver-past, I shall reach home at last, Heav'n is my home.
most and best, There, too, I soon shall rest, Heav'n is my home.

No. 204. I'LL BE THERE.

ISAAC WATTS.

Adapted by WM. J. KIRKPATRICK.

1. { There is a land of pure de-light, Where saints im-mor-tal reign; }
   { In-fi-nite day ex-cludes the night, And pleas-ures ban-ish pain. }
2. { There ev-er-last-ing spring a-bides, And nev-er-with'ring flow'rs; }
   { Death, like a nar-row sea, di-vides This heav'nly land from ours. }

CHORUS.

I'll be there, I'll be there, When the first trumpet sounds I'll be there,
I'll be there, I'll be there, I'll be there,

I'll be there, I'll be there, When the first trumpet sounds I'll be there,
I'll be there, I'll be there,

3 Sweet fields beyond the swelling flood
  Stand dressed in living green;
So to the Jews old Canaan stood,
  While Jordan rolled between.

4 Could we but climb where Moses stood,
  And view the landscape o'er,
Not Jordan's stream, nor death's cold
  Should fright us from the shore. |flood

HE SHIELDS FROM THE STORMS OF LIFE.

E. C. Macartney.

W. S. Weeden.

1. { The Saviour's arms are o-pened wide, He shields from the storms of life ; }
   { We fear no ill when by his side, He shields from the storms of life. }
2. { No mat-ter where his hand may lead, He shields from the storms of life ; }
   { His lov-ing care sup-plies our need, He shields from the storms of life. }

Chorus.

He shields from the storms of life, He shields from the storms of life ; We'll

praise him with an end-less song, He shields from the storms of life.

3 Though oft our steps have gone astray,
He shields from the storms of life ;
He brought us to the narrow way,
He shields from the storms of life.

4 He is our loving Guide and Friend,
He shields from the storms of life ;
He'll safely keep us to the end,
He shields from the storms of life.

No. 206.   **JESUS, LOVER OF MY SOUL.**

Charles Wesley.

S. B. Marsh.

FINE.

1. { Je - sus, lov - er of my soul, Let me to thy bo - som fly, }
   { While the near-er wa-ters roll, While the tempest still is high ! }

D.C.—Safe in - to the ha-ven guide, Oh, re-ceive my soul at last.

D.C.

Hide me, O my Sav-iour, hide, Till the storm of life is past ;

2 Other refuge have I none,
Hangs my helpless soul on thee ;
Leave, oh leave me not alone,
Still support and comfort me.
All my trust on thee is stayed,
All my help from thee I bring ;
Cover my defenseless head,
With the shadow of thy wing.

3 Thou, O Christ, art all I want ;
More than all in thee I find ;
Raise the fallen ! cheer the faint !
Heal the sick ! and lead the blind !
Just and holy is thy name,
I am all unrighteousness :
Vile and full of sin I am,
Thou art full of truth and grace.

No. 207. WE WOULD SEE JESUS.

ANNA B. WILT.   FELIX MENDELSSOHN.

1. We would see Je - sus—for the shadows lengthen A-cross this lit - tle landscape of our life;
2. We would see Je-sus—the great Rock Foundation, Whereon our feet were set with sovereign grace;
3. We would see Je - sus—other lights are pal-ing, Which for long years we have rejoiced to see:
4. We would see Jesus—this is all we're needing, Strength, joy, and willingness come with the sight.

We would see Je - sus our weak faith to strengthen, For the last wea - ri - ness—the final strife.
Not life, nor death, with all their ag-i - ta - tion, Can thence remove us, if we see His face.
The blessings of our pilgrimage are fail - ing, We would not mourn them, for we go to Thee.
We would see Je - sus, dy-ing, ris-en, plead-ing, Then welcome day, and farewell mortal night!

No. 208. JESUS, THE VERY THOUGHT.

Tr. EDWARD CASWALL.   JOHN B. DYKES.

1. Je - sus, the ver - y thought of Thee, With sweetness fills my breast; But sweeter far Thy
2. Nor voice can sing, nor heart can frame, Nor can the mem'ry find   A sweeter sound than
3. O Hope of ev - 'ry con-trite heart! O Joy of all the meek! To those who fall, how

face to see   And in Thy presence rest.
Thy blest name,   O Saviour of man-kind!
kind Thou art!   How good to those who seek!

4 But what to those who find? Ah! This,
  Nor tongue nor pen can show;
  The love of Jesus, what it is,
  None but His loved ones know.

5 Jesus, our only joy be Thou,
  As Thou our prize wilt be;
  Jesus, be Thou our glory now,
  And through eternity.

No. 209. JESUS CALLS US.

CECIL F. ALEXANDER.   W. H. JUDE.

1. Je - sus calls us: o'er the tu - mult Of our life's wild, rest - less sea,
2. Je - sus calls us from the wor-ship Of the vain world's gold - en store;
3. In our joys and in our sor - rows, Days of toil and hours of ease,
4. Je - sus calls us: by Thy mer - cies, Sav - iour, make us hear Thy call.

Day by day His sweet voice sound - eth, Say - ing, "Chris - tian, fol - low me."
From each i - dol that would keep us, Say - ing, "Chris - tian, love Me more."
Still He calls, in cares and pleas - ures, "That we love Him more than these."
Give our hearts to Thine o - be - dience, Serve and love Thee best of all.

No. 210. I WAS A WANDERING SHEEP.

HORATIUS BONAR.　　　　　　　　　　　JOHN ZUNDEL.

1. I was a wand'ring sheep, I did not love the fold, I did not love my Shepherd's voice,

D.S.—I did not love my Father's voice.

FINE.　　　　　　　　　　　　　D.S.

I would not be con-trolled: I was a way-ward child, I did not love my home,

I loved a-far to roam.

2 The Shepherd sought His sheep,
The Father sought His child;
He followed me o'er vale and hill,
O'er deserts waste and wild:
He found me nigh to death,
Famished, and faint, and lone;
He bound me with the bands of love,
He saved the wandering one.

3 Jesus my Shepherd is;
'Twas He that loved my soul,
'Twas He that washed me in His blood,
'Twas He that made me whole:
'Twas He that sought the lost,
That found the wandering sheep,
'Twas He that brought me to the fold,
'Tis He that still doth keep.

No. 211. I DO BELIEVE.

REV. CHARLES WESLEY.　　　　　　　Unknown.

1. A - las! and did my Sav-iour bleed? and did my Sov-'reign die?
2. Was it for crimes that I had done, He groan'd up-on the tree?
3. But drops of grief can ne'er re - pay the debt of love I owe:

Cho.—I do be - lieve, I now be - lieve That Je - sus died for me;
D.C.

Would He de - vote that sa - cred head, For such a worm as I?
A - maz-ing pit - y! grace un-known! And love be-yond de - gree!
Here, Lord, I give my - self to Thee, 'Tis all that I can do.

And thro' His blood, His pre-cious blood, I shall from sin be free.

No. 212. GLORY BE TO THE FATHER.

Gloria Patri.　　　　HENRY W. GREATOREX.

Glo - ry be to the Fa-ther, and to the Son, and to the Ho - ly Ghost; As it

was in the beginning, is now, and ever shall be, world without end; A - men, A - men.

No. 213. WHAT A FRIEND WE HAVE IN JESUS.

JOSEPH SCRIVEN.　　　　　　　　　　　　　CHARLES C. CONVERSE.

1. What a friend we have in Je - sus, All our sins and griefs to bear!
2. Have we tri - als and temp-ta - tions? Is there trouble an - ywhere?
3. Are we weak and heav-y - la - den, Cumbered with a load of care?

What a priv - i - lege to car - ry Ev - 'rything to God in prayer.
We should nev- er be dis - couraged, Take it to the Lord in prayer.
Pre- cious Saviour, still our ref - uge,—Take it to the Lord in prayer.

FINE.

D.S.—All because we do not car - ry Ev - 'rything to God in prayer.
D.S.—Je - sus knows our ev- 'ry weakness, Take it to the Lord in prayer.
D.S.—In his arms he'll take and shield thee, Thou wilt find a sol - ace there.

D.S.

Oh, what peace we oft - en for - feit, Oh, what needless pain we bear—
Can we find a Friend so faith - ful, Who will all our sorrows share?
Do thy friends despise, for-sake thee? Take it to the Lord in prayer;

Used by permission.

No. 214.　　　　　　　ROCK OF AGES.

A. M. TOPLADY.　　　TOPLADY. 7s, 6'　　　THOS. HASTINGS.

1. Rock of A - ges, cleft for me, Let me hide my- self in thee;
2. Could my tears for - ev - er flow, Could my zeal no languor know,
3. While I draw this fleet- ing breath, When my eyes shall close in death,

Let the wa - ter and the blood, From thy wound- ed side that flow'd,
These for sin could not a - tone; Thou must save, and thou a - lone;
When I rise to worlds unknown, And be - hold thee on thy throne,

Be of sin the doub - le cure, Save from wrath and make me pure.
In my hand no price I bring, Sim - ply to thy cross I cling.
Rock of A - ges, cleft for me, Let me hide my - self in thee.

No. 215. BEHOLD A STRANGER'S AT THE DOOR.

HENRY K. OLIVER.

1. Be-hold a Stranger's at the door! He gently knocks,has knock'd before;
2. Oh, love-ly at - ti - tude, He stands With melting heart and load-ed hands!
3. But will He prove a friend in-deed? He will; the ver - y friend you need:

Has wait-ed long— is wait-ing still; You treat no oth - er friend so ill.
Oh, matchless kindness! and He shows This matchless kindness to His foes;
The friend of sin - ners—yes, 'tis He, With garments dyed on Cal - va - ry.

4 Rise, touched with gratitude divine;
Turn out His enemy and thine,
That soul-destroying monster, sin,
And let the heavenly Stranger in.

5 Admit Him, ere His anger burn—
His feet departed, ne'er return:
Admit Him, or the hour's at hand
You'll at His door rejected stand.

No. 216.   JESUS, THY NAME I LOVE.

JAMES G. DECK.   JOSEPH P. HOLBROOK.

1. Je-sus,Thy name I love, All other names above, Je - sus,my Lord! Oh,Thou art
2. Thou, blessed Son of God, Hast bought me with Thy blood,Je-sus,my Lord! Oh,how great
3. When unto Thee I flee, Thou wilt my refuge be, Je-sus,my Lord! What need I
4. Soon Thou wilt come again! I shall be happy then, Jesus,my Lord! Then Thine own

all to me! Nothing to please I see Nothing apart from Thee, Je-sus, my Lord!
is Thy love, All oth-er loves above, Love that I dai-ly prove, Je-sus, my Lord!
now to fear? What earthly grief or care, Since Thou art ever near? Je-sus, my Lord!
face I'll see, Then I shall like Thee be, Then evermore with Thee, Je-sus, my Lord!

Used by permission.

No. 217.   ART THOU WEARY?

Tr. JOHN M. NEALE.   HENRY W. BAKER.

1. Art thou weary? art thou languid?
Art thou sore distrest?
"Come to Me," saith One, "and coming,
Be at rest !"

2 Hath He marks to lead me to Him,
If He be my guide?—
" In His feet and hands are wound-prints,
And His side."

3 If I find Him, if I follow,
What His guerdon here?—
" Many a sorrow, many a labor,
Many a tear."

4 If I still hold closely to Him,
What hath He at last?
" Sorrow vanquished, labor ended,
Jordan passed."

5 If I ask Him to receive me,
Will He say me nay?
" Not till earth, and not till heaven
Pass away."

No. 218. **THE LOVE OF THE SPIRIT.**

Rev. P. H. Brooks, D. D.   Francois H. Barthelemon.

1. Praise the "Love of God" "our Fa-ther," Praise the love of God His Son;
2. E - qual love from e-qual per-sons, Father's shines in *all He gives;*
3. Let the soul from sin re-turn-ing, Trust the Spir-it's love no less

Praise the love of God the Spir-it "Showing" Three such Loves *by One.*
Je - sus shone in *all He suf-fered,* And the Third *with-in us lives.*
Than th' Father's strongest yearn-ing; Or Christ's blood and righteousness.

Halt not with a sin-gle les-son, Of His warm and wondrous love;
Shall we be "endued with pow-er," As we pray in waiting bands?
What His love "saith to the churches" Greets us still, if we will hear.

Nes - tle deep - er, and still deep - er In our hearts, most gen-tle dove.
Be not slow to learn the se - cret, 'Tis *love's heart* that moves *love's hands.*
"Teaching," "searching," "filling," "sealing," "Helping," "Guiding," love so near.

No. 219. **HOLY GHOST.**

1. Ho - ly Ghost, the In - fi - nite! Shine up - on our na - ture's night
2. We are sin - ful, cleanse us, Lord; We are faint, Thy strength af - ford;
3. Like the dew thy peace dis - til; Guide, sub-due our way - ward will,
4. In us "Ab - ba, Fa - ther," cry, Earn - est of our bliss on high,

With Thy bless - ed in - ward light, Com - fort - er Di - vine!
Lost, un - til by Thee re - stored, Com - fort - er Di - vine!
Things of Christ un - fold - ing still, Com - fort - er Di - vine!
Seal of im - mor - tal - i - ty Com - fort - er Di - vine!

No. 220. MASTER, I HAVE HEARD THEE PLEADING.

E. H. J.   J. MOUNTAIN.

1. Master, I have heard thee pleading With my inmost soul to-night! Now thy solemn
2. Spir-it, soul, and body yielding Will-ing-ly to thee, my Lord! What I give thou
3. Now, henceforth, Lord, and forever, I am thine, yes, all for thee; Thine in service,

CHO.—Jesus, Master, search me, prove me! With thy fire try my heart; All I am and

FINE. p

mes-sage heeding, I would end the fight: Vain-ly hath my soul been struggling
now art tak-ing: I be-lieve thy word! Yes! I trust thee as my Keep-er,
or in suff'ring—Chose my path for me. Peace and joy my heart are fill - ing;

have I yield, Lord; All I need—thou art.

rit.   *p*   *Chorus. D.C.*

With the tyrant on its throne; Now, dear Lord, the kingdom taking, Claim me thine alone.
'Mid temptations day by day, Trust thee as my Guide and Leader In the narrow way.
Rest beyond all pow'r to tell, This my ever-deep'ning portion While in thee I dwell.

No. 221.   NOW THE DAY IS OVER.

SABINE BARING-GOULD.   JOSEPH BARNBY.

1. Now the day is   o - ver,   Night is draw - ing   nigh,
2. Je - sus, give the   wea - ry   Calm and sweet re -   pose;
3. Grant to lit - tle   chil - dren   Vis - ions bright of   thee;
4. Thro' the long night-watch - es,   May thine an - gels   spread
5. When the morning wak - ens,   Then may I   a -   rise,

Shad - ows of the   even - ing   Steal a - cross the   sky.
With thy tend-'rest bless - ing   May our eye - lids close.
Guard the sail - ors   toss - ing   On   the deep blue   sea.
Their white wings a - bove me,   Watch - ing round my bed.
Pure and fresh and   sin - less   In   thy ho - ly   eyes.

Steal a - cross   the   sky.

No. 222.　　I NEED THEE, PRECIOUS JESUS.

FREDERICK WHITFIELD.　　　　　　　　　　　　SAMUEL WESLEY.

1. I need Thee, precious Jesus! For I am full of sin; My soul is dark and
2. I need Thee, blessed Jesus! For I am ver-y poor; A stranger and a
3. I need Thee, blessed Jesus! And hope to see Thee soon, Encircled with the

guilt - y, My heart is dead within ; I need the cleansing fountain, Where
pilgrim, I have no earthly store; I need the love of Je - sus To
rainbow, And seated on Thy throne : There, with Thy blood-bought children, My

I can always flee, The blood of Christ most precious, The sinner's perfect plea.
cheer me on my way, To guide my doubting footsteps, To be my strength and stay.
joy shall ever be To sing Thy praise, Lord Jesus, To gaze, my Lord, on Thee!

No. 223.　　　ABIDE WITH ME.

HENRY F. LYTE.　　　　　　　　　　　　WILLIAM HENRY MONK.

1. A - bide with me: fast falls the e - ven - tide; The dark - ness
2. Swift to its close ebbs out life's lit - tle day; Earth's joys grow
3. I need Thy pres - ence ev - 'ry pass-ing hour; What but Thy
4. I fear no foe, with Thee at hand to bless; Ills have no

deep - ens; Lord, with me a - bide! When oth - er help - ers
dim, its glo - ries pass a - way; Change and de - cay in
grace can foil the temp-ter's power? Who, like Thy - self, my
weight, and tears no bit - ter - ness; Where is death's sting? where,

fail, and com-forts flee, Help of the help-less, O a - bide with me!
all a - round I see; O Thou, who changest not a - bide with me!
guide and stay can be? Thro' cloud and sunshine, Lord, a - bide with me!
grave, Thy vic - to - ry? I triumph still, if Thou a - bide with me.

ISAAC WATTS.　　　　　　　　　　JOHN HATTON.

1. From all that dwell be - low the skies, Let the Cre - a - tor's praise a - rise;
2. E - ter-nal are Thy mer - cies, Lord; E - ter-nal truth at - tends Thy word;

Let the Re - deem-er's name be sung Thro' ev-'ry land, by ev-'ry tongue.
Thy praise shall sound from shore to shore Till suns shall rise and set no more.

No. 225. Jesus Shall Reign. L. M.

1 Jesus shall reign where'er the sun
　Does his successive journeys run;
　His kingdom stretch from shore to shore,
　Till moons shall wax and wane no more.

2 From north to south the princes meet
　To pay their homage at His feet;
　While western empires own their Lord,
　And savage tribes attend His word.

3 To Him shall endless prayer be made,
　And endless praises crown His head;
　His name, like sweet perfume, shall rise
　With every morning sacrifice.

4 People and realms, of every tongue,
　Dwell on His love with sweetest song,
　And infant voices shall proclaim
　Their early blessings on His name.
　　　　　　　　　　ISAAC WATTS.

No. 226. Glorying in the Cross. L. M.

1 When I survey the wondrous cross
　On which the Prince of glory died,
　My richest gain I count but loss,
　And pour contempt on all my pride.

2 Forbid it, Lord, that I should boast,
　Save in the death of Christ, my God;
　All the vain things that charm me most,
　I sacrifice them to His blood.

3 See, from His head, His hands, His feet,
　Sorrow and love flow mingled down!
　Did e'er such love and sorrow meet?
　Or thorns compose so rich a crown?

4 Were the whole realm of nature mine,
　That were a present far too small;
　Love so amazing, so divine,
　Demands my soul, my life, my all.
　　　　　　　　　　ISAAC WATTS.

HAMBURG. L. M.

Arr. by LOWELL MASON.

No. 227. Lord, I Am Thine. L. M.

1 Lord, I am Thine, entirely Thine,
　Purchased and saved by blood divine;
　With full consent Thine would I be,
　And own Thy sovereign right in me.

2 Thine would I live, Thine would I die,
　Be Thine through all eternity;
　The vow is past, beyond repeal,
　Now will I set the solemn seal.

3 Here, at that cross where flows the blood
　That bought my guilty soul for God,
　Thee, my new Master, now I call,
　And consecrate to Thee my all.

4 Do Thou assist a feeble worm
　The great engagement to perform;
　Thy grace can full assistance lend,
　And on that grace I dare depend.
　　　　　　　　　　SAMUEL DAVIES.

No. 228. Not Ashamed of Jesus. L. M.

1 Jesus! and shall it ever be,
　A mortal man ashamed of Thee?
　Ashamed of Thee, whom angels praise,
　Whose glories shine thro' endless days?

2 Ashamed of Jesus! sooner far
　Let evening blush to own a star:
　He sheds the beams of light divine
　O'er this benighted soul of mine.

3 Ashamed of Jesus! just as soon
　Let midnight be ashamed of noon:
　'Tis midnight with my soul till He,
　Bright Morning Star, bid darkness flee.

4 Ashamed of Jesus! that dear Friend,
　On whom my hopes of heaven depend?
　No: when I blush, be this my shame,
　That I no more revere His name.
　　　　　　　　　　JOSEPH GRIGG.

No. 229. ARLINGTON. C. M.

CHARLES WESLEY.

THOMAS A. ARNE.

1. O   for   a heart to praise my God,   A heart from sin   set   free,
2. A   heart resigned, sub-mis-sive, meek, My great Re-deem-er's   throne,
3. O   for   a low-ly,   con-trite heart, Be-liev-ing, true, and   clean,
4. A   heart in ev-'ry thought renewed, And full of love di-   vine;

A heart that al-ways feels Thy blood, So free-ly spilt for   me!
Where on-ly Christ is heard to speak, Where Je-sus reigns a-   lone.
Which nei-ther life nor death can part From Him that dwells with-in!
Per-fect, and right, and pure, and good— A cup-y, Lord, of   Thine.

No. 230. O FOR A FAITH. C. M.

1 O for a faith that will not shrink,
   Though pressed by ev'ry foe,
   That will not tremble on the brink
   Of any earthly woe!

2 That will not murmur nor complain
   Beneath the chastening rod,
   But, in the hour of grief or pain,
   Will lean upon its God;

3 A faith that shines more bright and clear
   When tempests rage without;
   That when in danger knows no fear,
   In darkness feels no doubt;

4 Lord, give us such a faith as this;
   And then, whate'er may come,
   We'll taste, e'en here, the hallowed bliss
   Of an eternal home.

WILLIAM HILEY BATHURST.

No. 231. AM I A SOLDIER. C. M.

1 Am I a soldier of the cross,
   A foll'wer of the Lamb,
   And shall I fear to own His cause,
   Or blush to speak His name?

2 Must I be carried to the skies
   On flowery beds of ease,
   While others fought to win the prize,
   And sailed through bloody seas?

3 Are there no foes for me to face?
   Must I not stem the flood?
   Is this vile world a friend to grace,
   To help me on to God?

4 Sure I must fight if I would reign;
   Increase my courage, Lord:
   I'll bear the toil, endure the pain,
   Supported by Thy word.

ISAAC WATTS.

AZMON. C. M.

C. G. GLASER.

No. 232. Forever Here my Rest. C. M.

1 Forever here my rest shall be,
   Close to Thy bleeding side;
   This all my hope, and all my plea,
   For me the Saviour died.

2 My dying Saviour and my God,
   Fountain for guilt and sin,
   Sprinkle me ever with Thy blood,
   And cleanse and keep me clean.

3 Wash me, and make me thus Thine own;
   Wash me, and mine Thou art;
   Wash me, but not my feet alone,—
   My hands, my head, my heart.

4 Th' atonement of Thy blood apply,
   Till faith to sight improve;
   Till hope in full fruition die,
   And all my soul be love.

CHARLES WESLEY.

No. 233. The Dearest Name. C. M.

1 How sweet the name of Jesus sounds
   In a believer's ear!
   It soothes his sorrows, heals his wounds,
   And drives away his fear.

2 It makes the wounded spirit whole,
   And calms the troubled breast;
   'Tis manna to the hungry soul,
   And to the weary, rest.

3 Dear Name, the rock on which I build,
   My shield and hiding-place;
   My never-failing treasury, filled
   With boundless stores of grace.

4 Jesus, my Shepherd, Saviour, Friend,
   My Prophet, Priest, and King;
   My Lord, my Life, my Way, my End,
   Accept the praise I bring!

JOHN NEWTON.

No. 234. HOW PRECIOUS IS THE BOOK DIVINE.

BELMONT. C. M.

JOHN FAWCETT.　　　　　　　　　　　　Fr. WILLIAM GARDINER.

1. How pre-cious is the book di-vine, By in-spi-ra-tion given!
2. Its light de-scend-ing from a-bove, Our gloomy world to cheer,
3. It shows to man his wand'ring ways, And where his feet have trod;

Bright as a lamp its doctrines shine, To guide our souls to heav'n.
Displays a Sav-iour's boundless love, And brings his glo-ries near.
And brings to view the matchless grace Of a for-giv-ing God.

4 O'er all the strait and narrow way
Its radiant beams are cast;
A light whose never weary ray
Grows brightest at the last.

5 It sweetly cheers our fainting hearts
In this dark vale of tears;
Life, light, and comfort it imparts,
And calms our anxious fears.

6 This lamp through all the dreary night
Of life shall guide our way,
Till we behold the clearer light
Of an eternal day.

No. 235. THE SPIRIT BREATHES.

1 The Spirit breathes upon the word,
And brings the truth to sight;
Precepts and promises afford
A sanctifying light.

2 A glory gilds the sacred page,
Majestic, like the sun;
It gives a light to every age;—
It gives, but borrows none.

3 The hand, that gave it, still supplies
The gracious light and heat;—
Its truths upon the nations rise,—
They rise, but never set,

4 Let everlasting thanks be thine,
For such a bright display,
As makes a world of darkness shine
With beams of heavenly day.

5 My soul rejoices to pursue
The steps of him I love,
Till glory breaks upon my view,
In brighter worlds above.

William Cowper.

No. 236. FATHER OF MERCIES.

1 Father of mercies! in thy word
What endless glory shines!
For ever be thy name adored,
For these celestial lines.

2 Here, the fair tree of knowledge grows
And yields a free repast;
Sublimer sweets than nature knows
Invite the longing taste.

3 Here, the Redeemer's welcome voice
Spreads heavenly peace around;
And life and everlasting joys
Attend the blissful sound.

4 Oh, may these heavenly pages be
My ever dear delight;
And still new beauties may I see,
And still increasing light.

Anne Steele.

MY JESUS, AS THOU WILT.

C. M. VON WEBER.

1. My Je-sus, as thou wilt; Oh, may thy will be mine; In-to thy hand of love
2. My Je-sus, as thou wilt; Tho' seen thro' many a tear, Let not my star of hope
3. My Je-sus, as thou wilt; All shall be well with me, Each changing future scene,

I would my all re-sign; Thro' sor-row or thro' joy, Con-duct me
Grow dim or dis-ap-pear; Since thou on earth hast wept, And sor-rowed
I glad-ly trust with thee; Straight to my home a-bove, I trav-el

as thine own, And help me still to say, "My Lord, thy will be done."
oft a-lone, If I must weep with thee, My Lord, thy will be done.
calm-ly on, And sing in life or death,—My Lord, thy will be done.

LEAD, KINDLY LIGHT.

J. B. DYKES.

No. 238. LEAD, KINDLY LIGHT.

1 Lead, kindly Light, amid th' encircling gloom,
  Lead thou me on;
The night is dark, and I am far from home,
  Lead thou me on.
Keep thou my feet; I do not ask to see
The distant scene; one step enough for me.

2 I was not ever thus, nor prayed that thou
  Shouldst lead me on;
I loved to choose and see my path; but now
  Lead thou me on.
I loved the garish day, and, spite of fears,
Pride ruled my will: remember not past years.

3 So long thy power hath blessed me, sure it still
  Will lead me on
O'er moor and fen, o'er crag and torrent, till
  The night is gone,
And with the morn those angel faces smile,
Which I have loved long since, and lost awhile.

John H. Newman.

No. 239. THY WORD, O LORD.
(Tune above.)

1 Thy word, O Lord, thy precious word alone,
  Can lead me on;
By this, until the darksome night be gone,
  Lead thou me on!
Thy word is light, thy word is life and pow'r,
By it, oh, guide me in each trying hour!

2 Whate'er my path, led by the word, 'tis good,
  Oh, lead me on!
Be my poor heart thy blessed word's abode,
  Lead thou me on!
Thy Holy Spirit gives the light to see,
And leads me by thy word close following thee.

3 Led by aught else, I tread a devious way,
  Oh, lead me on!
Speak, Lord, and help me ever to obey,
  Lead thou me on!
My every step shall then be well defined,
And all I do according to thy mind.

Albert Midlane.

ST. AGNES. C. M.

ISAAC WATTS.   JOHN B. DYKES.

1. Lo! what a glo-rious sight ap-pears   To our be-liev-ing eyes!
2. From the third heaven where God resides—That ho-ly, hap-py place,—
3. At-tend-ing an-gels shout for joy,   And the bright ar-mies sing,—

The earth and seas are passed a-way,   And the old roll-ing skies.
The New Je-ru-sa-lem comes down,   Adorned with shin-ing grace.
"Mortals! be-hold the sa-cred seat   Of your de-scend-ing King:—

---

4 "The God of glory, down to men,
Removes his blest abode;
Men, the dear objects of his grace,
And he their loving God:—

5 "His own soft hand shall wipe the tears
From every weeping eye;   [fears,
And pains, and groans, and grief, and
And death itself shall die!"

6 How long, dear Saviour! O! how long
Shall this bright hour delay?
Fly swifter round, ye wheels of time!
And bring the welcome day.

No. 241. LIGHT OF THE LONELY.

1 Light of the lonely pilgrim's heart!
Star of the coming day!
Arise, and with thy morning beams
Chase all our griefs away.

2 Come, blesséd Lord! let every shore
And answering island sing
The praises of thy royal name,
And own thee as their king.

3 Hope of our hearts, O Lord, appear,
Thou glorious Star of day!
Shine forth and chase the dreary night,
With all our tears away.

4 No resting-place we seek on earth,
No loveliness we see;
Our eye is on the royal crown,
Prepared for us—and thee!

5 But, dearest Lord, however bright,
That crown of joy above,
What is it to the brighter hope
Of dwelling in thy love?
Edward Denny.

No. 242. BRIDE OF THE LAMB.

1 Bride of the Lamb, awake, awake!
Why sleep for sorrow now?
The hope of glory, Christ, is thine,
A child of glory, thou.

2 Thy spirit, through the lonely night,
From earthly joy apart,
Hath sighed for one that's far away,—
The Bridegroom of thy heart.

3 But see! the night is waning fast,
The breaking morn is near;
And Jesus comes with voice of love,
Thy drooping heart to cheer.

4 Then weep no more; 'tis all thine own,
His crown, his joy divine;
And, sweeter far than all beside,
He, be himself is thine!
Edward Denny.

LOUVAN. L. M.

Anon.　　　　　　　　Ps. 23.　　　　　　　Virgil C. Taylor.

1. My Shepherd is the Lord Most High, And all my wants shall be supplied:

In pastures green he makes me lie, And leads by streams which gently glide.

2 He in his mercy doth restore
　My soul when sinking in distress;
　For his name's sake he evermore
　Leads me in paths of righteousness.

3 Yea, tho' I walk thro' death's dark vale,
　E'en there no evil will I fear,
　Because thy presence shall not fail,
　Thy rod and staff my soul shall cheer.

4 For me a table thou hast spread,
　Prepared before the face of foes;
　With oil thou dost anoint my head;
　My cup is filled and overflows.

No. 244. COMPLETE IN THEE.

1 Complete in thee, no work of mine
　May take, dear Lord, the place of thine;
　Thy blood has pardon bought for me,
　And I am now complete in thee.

2 Complete in thee—no more shall sin
　Thy grace has conquered, reign within;
　Thy voice will bid the tempter flee,
　And I shall stand complete in thee.

3 Complete in thee—each want supplied,
　And no good thing to me denied,
　Since thou my portion, Lord, wilt be,
　I ask no more—complete in thee.

4 Complete in thee, for ever blest,
　Of all thy fullness, Lord, possessed,
　Thy praise throughout eternity—
　Thy love I'll sing complete in thee.
　　　　　　　　　　　　Aaron R. Wolfe.

No. 245. MY SOUL COMPLETE.

1 My soul complete in Jesus stands!
　It fears no more the law's demands;
　The smile of God is sweet within,
　Where all before was guilt and sin.

2 My soul at rest in Jesus lives;
　Accepts the peace his pardon gives;
　Receives the grace his death secured,
　And pleads the anguish he endured.

3 My soul its every foe defies,
　And cries—'Tis God that justifies!
　Who charges God's elect with sin?
　Shall Christ, who died their peace to win?

4 A song of praise my soul shall sing,
　To our eternal, glorious King!
　Shall worship humbly at his feet,
　In whom alone it stands complete.
　　　　　　　　　　　Grace W. Hinsdale.

No. 246. LET ME HEAR.

1 Let me hear my Saviour say,
　"Strength shall be equal to thy day;"
　Then I rejoice in deep distress,
　Leaning on all-sufficient grace.

2 I can do all things—or can bear
　All suffering, if my Lord be there;
　Sweet pleasures mingle with the pains,
　While he my sinking head sustains.

3 I glory in infirmity,
　That Christ's own power may rest on me;
　When I am weak, then am I strong;
　Grace is my shield, and Christ my song.
　　　　　　　　　　　　　Isaac Watts.

No. 247.

LO! HE COMES.

ZION. 8s, 7s, 4.

CHARLES WESLEY, alt.

THOMAS HASTINGS.

1. Lo, he comes, with clouds descending, Once for favored sinners slain ; Thousand thousand saints at-tend-ing Swell the triumph of his train ; Hal - le - lu-jah ! God appears on earth to reign ; Hal-le - lu-jah ! God appears on earth to reign.

2 Every eye shall now behold him,
  Robed in dreadful majesty ;
Those who set at naught and sold him,
Pierced, and nailed him to the tree,
  Deeply wailing,
Shall the true Messiah see.

3 Yea, Amen ; let all adore thee,
  High on thine eternal throne:
Saviour, take the power and glory ;
Claim the kingdom for thine own.
  Oh, come quickly,
Hallelujah ! Come, Lord, come.

No. 248. HE COMETH!

Tune.—"Old Black Joe." Key of D.

1 Bright breaks the morn,
  The night is almost o'er ;
Fair glows the dawn
  On Canaan's blissful shore.
Faith, lost in sight
  Shall reap her full reward ;
O, trim your lamps, and wait the coming
  Of the Lord!

REFRAIN.

He's coming ! He's coming !
  Are you ready for that day?
O, trim your lamps and set them burning !
  Watch and pray !

2 Not as of old,
  In poor and lowly guise ;
Cometh the king
  In glory from the skies ;
Angels and saints
  In countless hosts attend
When Jesus from his throne in heaven
  Shall descend.

3 E'en as he rose,
  In clouds that veiled his light
So shall he come,
  To end the world's dark night:
"Coming in clouds!"
  The angel's promise rings ;
The Sun of Righteousness with healing
  In his wings!

Flora Kirkland.

No. 249.   **DENNIS. S. M.**

ALBERT MIDLANE.

H. G. NÄGELI.

1. Re - vive thy work, O Lord, Thy might - y arm make bare;
2. Re - vive thy work, O Lord, Cre :- ate soul - thirst for Thee;
3. Re - vive thy work, O Lord, Ex - alt Thy pre - cious name;

Speak with the voice that wakes the dead, And make thy peo - ple hear.
And hung'r-ing for the Bread of Life, O may our spir - its be!
And by the Ho - ly Ghost, our love For Thee and Thine in-flame.

No. 250. BLEST BE THE TIE. S. M.

1 Blest be the tie that binds
  Our hearts in Christian love:
  The following of kindred minds
  Is like to that above.

2 Before our Father's throne
  We pour our ardent prayers;
  Our fears, our hopes, our aims are one,
  Our comforts and our cares.

3 We share our mutual woes,
  Our mutual burdens bear;
  And often for each other flows
  The sympathizing tear.

4 When we asunder part,
  It gives us inward pain;
  But we shall still be joined in heart,
  And hope to meet again.

JOHN FAWCETT.

No. 251. A CHARGE TO KEEP. S. M.

1 A charge to keep I have,
  A God to glorify;
  A never-dying soul to save,
  And fit it for the sky.

2 To serve the present age,
  My calling to fulfill,
  O may it all my powers engage,
  To do my Master's will!

3 Arm me with jealous care,
  As in Thy sight to live;
  And O, thy servant, Lord, prepare
  A strict account to give!

4 Help me to watch and pray,
  And on thyself rely,
  Assured, if I my trust betray,
  I shall forever die.

CHAS. WESLEY.

BOYLSTON. S. M.

LOWELL MASON.

No. 252. And Can I Yet Delay. S. M.

1 And can I yet delay
  My little all to give?
  To tear my soul from earth away
  For Jesus to receive?

2 Nay, but I yield, I yield!
  I can hold out no more:
  I sink, by dying love compelled,
  And own Thee conqueror!

3 Though late, I all forsake;
  My friends, my all resign:
  Gracious Redeemer, take, O take,
  And seal me ever Thine.

4 Come, and possess me whole,
  Nor hence again remove:
  Settle and fix my wav'ring soul
  With all thy weight of love.

CHAS. WESLEY.

No. 253. Evils of Intemperance. S. M.

1 Mourn for the thousands slain,
  The youthful and the strong;
  Mourn for the wine cup's fearful reign
  And the deluded throng.

2 Mourn for the ruined soul—
  Eternal life and light
  Lost by the fiery, maddening bowl,
  And turned to hopeless night.

3 Mourn for the lost;—but call,
  Call to the strong, the free:
  Rouse them to shun that dreadful fall,
  And to the refuge flee.

4 Mourn for the lost;—but pray,
  Pray to our God above,
  To break the fell destroyer's sway,
  And show His saving love.

No. 254. GOD BE WITH YOU!

"The grace of our Lord Jesus Christ be with you."—Romans 16: 20.

JEREMIAH E. RANKIN. WILLIAM G. TOMER.

1. God be with you till we meet a - gain!— By his counsels guide, up-
2. God be with you till we meet a - gain!—'Neath his wings protecting
3. God be with you till we meet a - gain!—When life's perils thick con-
4. God be with you till we meet a - gain!—Keep love's banner floating

hold   you,   With his sheep se-cure-ly fold   you;   God   be
hide   you,   Dai - ly man-na still di - vide you;   God   be
found   you,   Put his arms un-fail-ing round you;   God   be
o'er   you,   Smite death's threat'ning wave before you; God   be

with you till   we meet a - gain!
with you till   we meet a - gain!
with you till   we meet a - gain!   } Till we meet!   Till we
with you till   we meet a - gain!

CHORUS.

Till we meet! Till we

meet!   Till we meet   at Je - sus' feet;   Till   we
meet a - gain!   Till we meet!

meet!...... Till we meet! God be with you till we meet a - gain!
Till we meet! Till we meet a-gain!

THE TEN COMMANDMENTS.

1. Thou shalt have no other gods before me.

2. Thou shalt not make unto thee any graven image, or any likeness of any thing that is in heaven above, or that is in the earth beneath, or that is in the water under the earth: thou shalt not bow down thyself to them, nor serve them: for I the Lord thy God am a jealous God, visiting the iniquity of the fathers upon the children unto the third and fourth generation of them that hate me; and showing mercy unto thousands of them that love me, and keep my commandments.

3. Thou shalt not take the name of the Lord thy God in vain: for the Lord will not hold him guiltless that taketh his name in vain.

4. Remember the Sabbath day, to keep it holy. Six days shalt thou labor, and do all thy work: but the seventh day is the Sabbath of the Lord thy God: in it thou shalt not do any work, thou, nor thy son, nor thy daughter, thy manservant, nor thy maidservant, nor thy cattle, nor thy stranger that is within thy gates: for in six days the Lord made heaven and earth, the sea, and all that in them is, and rested the seventh day: wherefore the Lord blessed the Sabbath day, and hallowed it.

5. Honor thy father and thy mother: that thy days may be long upon the land which the Lord thy God giveth thee.

6. Thou shalt not kill.

7. Thou shalt not commit adultery.

8. Thou shalt not steal.

9. Thou shalt not bear false witness against thy neighbor.

10. Thou shalt not covet thy neighbor's house, thou shalt not covet thy neighbor's wife, nor his manservant, nor his maidservant, nor his ox, nor his ass, nor anything that is thy neighbor's.—Ex. 20: 3-17.

THE APOSTLES' CREED.

I believe in God the Father Almighty, Maker of heaven and earth. And in Jesus Christ his only begotten Son our Lord: who was conceived by the Holy Ghost, born of the Virgin Mary; suffered under Pontius Pilate, was crucified, dead and buried; he descended into hades; the third day he rose from the dead; he ascended into heaven; and sitteth at the right hand of God the Father Almighty; from thence he shall come to judge the quick and the dead. I believe in the Holy Ghost; the holy catholic Church, the communion of saints, the forgiveness of sins; the resurrection of the body, and the life everlasting. Amen.

No. 255. OLD HUNDRED. L. M.

THOMAS KEN.   GUILLAUME FRANC.

Praise God, from whom all blessings flow, Praise him, all creatures here below;

Praise him a-bove, ye heavenly host; Praise Father, Son, and Ho-ly Ghost!

210

RESPONSIVE SCRIPTURE READINGS.

SELECTION 1.

PSALM 1.

1 Blessed is the man that walketh not in the counsel of the ungodly, nor standeth in the way of sinners, nor sitteth in the seat of the scornful.

2 But his delight is in the law of the Lord; and in his law doth he meditate day and night.

3 And he shall be like a tree planted by the rivers of water, that bringeth forth his fruit in his season; his leaf also shall not wither; and whatsoever he doeth shall prosper.

4 The ungodly are not so: but are like the chaff which the wind driveth away.

5 Therefore the ungodly shall not stand in the judgment, nor sinners in the congregation of the righteous.

6 For the Lord knoweth the way of the righteous: but the way of the ungodly shall perish.

PSALM 2.

1 Why do the heathen rage, and the people imagine a vain thing?

2 The kings of the earth set themselves, and the rulers take counsel together, against the Lord, and against his Anointed, saying,

3 Let us break their bands asunder, and cast away their cords from us.

4 He that sitteth in the heavens shall laugh: the Lord shall have them in derision.

5 Then shall he speak unto them in his wrath, and vex them in his sore displeasure.

6 Yet have I set my king upon my holy hill of Zion.

7 I will declare the decree: the Lord hath said unto me, Thou art my Son; this day have I begotten thee.

8 Ask of me, and I shall give thee the heathen for thine inheritance, and the uttermost parts of the earth for thy possession.

9 Thou shalt break them with a rod of iron; thou shalt dash them in pieces like a potter's vessel.

10 Be wise now therefore, O ye kings: be instructed, ye judges of the earth.

11 Serve the Lord with fear, and rejoice with trembling.

12 Kiss the Son, lest he be angry, and ye perish from the way, when his wrath is kindled but a little. Blessed are all they that put their trust in him.

PSALM 3.

1 Lord, how are they increased that trouble me! Many are they that rise up against me.

2 Many there be which say of my soul, There is no help for him in God.

3 But thou, O Lord, art a shield for me; my glory, and the lifter up of mine head.

4 I cried unto the Lord with my voice, and he heard me out of his holy hill.

5 I laid me down and slept; I awaked; for the Lord sustained me.

6 I will not be afraid of ten thousands of people, that have set themselves against me round about.

7 Arise, O Lord; save me, O my God: for thou hast smitten all mine enemies upon the cheek bone; thou hast broken the teeth of the ungodly.

8 Salvation belongeth unto the Lord: thy blessing is upon thy people.

209

SELECTION 2

PSALM 32.

1 Blessed is he whose transgression is forgiven, whose sin is covered.

2 Blessed is the man unto whom the Lord imputeth not iniquity, and in whose spirit there is no guile.

3 When I kept silence, my bones waxed old through my roaring all the day long.

4 For day and night thy hand was heavy upon me: my moisture is turned into the drought of summer. Selah.

5 I acknowledged my sin unto thee, and mine iniquity have I not hid. I said, I will confess my transgressions unto the Lord; and thou forgavest the iniquity of my sin. Selah.

6 For this shall every one that is godly pray unto thee in a time when thou mayest be found: surely in the floods of great waters they shall not come nigh unto him.

7 Thou art my hiding place; thou shalt preserve me from trouble; thou shalt compass me about with songs of deliverance. Selah.

8 I will instruct thee and teach thee in the way which thou shalt go: I will guide thee with mine eye.

9 Be ye not as the horse, or as the mule, which have no understanding: whose mouth must be held in with bit and bridle, lest they come near unto thee.

10 Many sorrows shall be to the wicked, but he that trusteth in the Lord, mercy shall compass him about.

11 Be glad in the Lord, and rejoice, ye righteous: and shout for joy, all ye that are upright in heart.

SELECTION 3.

PSALM 34.

1 I will bless the Lord at all times: his praise shall continually be in my mouth.

2 My soul shall make her boast in the Lord: the humble shall hear thereof, and be glad.

3 O magnify the Lord with me, and let us exalt his name together.

4 I sought the Lord, and he heard me, and delivered me from all my fears.

5 They looked unto him, and were lightened: and their faces were not ashamed.

6 This poor man cried, and the Lord heard him, and saved him out of all his troubles.

7 The angel of the Lord encampeth round about them that fear him, and delivereth them.

8 O taste and see that the Lord is good: blessed is the man that trusteth in him.

9 O fear the Lord, ye his saints: for there is no want to them that fear him.

10 The young lions do lack, and suffer hunger: but they that seek the Lord shall not want any good thing.

11 Come, ye children, hearken unto me: I will teach you the fear of the Lord.

12 What man is he that desireth life, and loveth many days, that he may see good?

13 Keep thy tongue from evil, and thy lips from speaking guile.

14 Depart from evil, and do good; seek peace, and pursue it.

15 The eyes of the Lord are upon the righteous, and his ears are open unto their cry.

16 The face of the Lord is against them that do evil, to cut off the remembrance of them from the earth.

17 The righteous cry, and the Lord heareth, and delivereth them out of all their troubles.

18 The Lord is nigh unto them that are of a broken heart; and saveth such as be of a contrite spirit.

19 Many are the afflictions of the righteous: but the Lord delivereth him out of them all.

20 He keepeth all his bones: not one of them is broken.

21 Evil shall slay the wicked: and they that hate the righteous shall be desolate.

PSALM 46.

1 God is our refuge and strength, a very present help in trouble.

2 Therefore will not we fear, though the earth be removed, and though the mountains be carried into the midst of the sea;

3 Though the waters thereof roar and be troubled, though the mountains shake with the swelling thereof.

4 There is a river, the streams whereof shall make glad the city of God, the holy place of the tabernacles of the Most High.

5 God is in the midst of her; she shall not be moved: God shall help her, and that right early.

6 The heathen raged, the kingdoms were moved: he uttered his voice, the earth melted.

7 The Lord of hosts is with us; the God of Jacob is our refuge.

8 Come, behold the works of the Lord, what desolations he hath made in the earth.

9 He maketh wars to cease unto the end of the earth; he breaketh the bow and cutteth the spear in sunder; he burneth the chariot in the fire.

10 Be still, and know that I am God: I will be exalted among the heathen, I will be exalted in the earth.

11 The Lord of hosts is with us; the God of Jacob is our refuge.

SELECTION 4.

PSALM 47.

1 O clap your hands, all ye people; shout unto God with the voice of triumph.

2 For the Lord most high is terrible; he is a great King over all the earth.

3 He shall subdue the people under us, and the nations under our feet.

4 He shall choose our inheritance for us, the excellency of Jacob whom he loved.

5 God is gone up with a shout, the Lord with the sound of a trumpet.

6 Sing praises to God, sing praises: sing praises unto our King, sing praises.

7 For God is the King of all the earth: sing ye praises with understanding.

8 God reigneth over the heathen: God sitteth upon the throne of his holiness.

9 The princes of the people are gathered together, even the people of the God of Abraham: for the shields of the earth belong unto God: he is greatly exalted.

PSALM 48.

1 Great is the Lord, and greatly to be praised in the city of our God, in the mountain of his holiness.

2 Beautiful for situation, the joy of the whole earth, is mount Zion, on the sides of the north, the city of the great King.

3 God is known in her palaces for a refuge.

4 For, lo, the kings were assembled, they passed by together.

5 They saw it, and so they marvelled; they were troubled, and hasted away.

6 Fear took hold upon them there, and pain, as of a woman in travail.

7 Thou breakest the ships of Tarshish with an east wind.

8 As we have heard, so have we seen in the city of the Lord of hosts, in the city of our God: God will establish it for ever.

9 We have thought of thy lovingkindness, O God, in the midst of thy temple.

10 According to thy name, O God, so is thy praise unto the ends of the earth: thy right hand is full of righteousness.

11 Let mount Zion rejoice, let the daughters of Judah be glad, because of thy judgments.

12 Walk about Zion, and go round about her: tell the towers thereof.

13 Mark ye well her bulwarks, consider her palaces; that ye may tell it to the generation following.

14 For this God is our God for ever and ever: he will be our guide even unto death.

SELECTION 5.

Psalm 51.

1 Have mercy upon me, O God, according to thy lovingkindness: according unto the multitude of thy tender mercies blot out my transgressions.

2 Wash me throughly from mine iniquity, and cleanse me from my sin.

3 For I acknowledge my transgressions: and my sin is ever before me.

4 Against thee, thee only, have I sinned, and done this evil in thy sight: that thou mightest be justified when thou speakest, and be clear when thou judgest.

5 Behold, I was shapen in iniquity; and in sin did my mother conceive me.

6 Behold, thou desirest truth in the inward parts: and in the hidden part thou shalt make me to know wisdom.

7 Purge me with hyssop, and I shall be clean: wash me, and I shall be whiter than snow.

8 Make me to hear joy and gladness; that the bones which thou hast broken may rejoice.

9 Hide thy face from my sins, and blot out all mine iniquities.

10 Create in me a clean heart, O God; and renew a right spirit within me.

11 Cast me not away from thy presence; and take not thy Holy Spirit from me.

12 Restore unto me the joy of thy salvation; and uphold me with thy free Spirit.

13 Then will I teach transgressors thy ways; and sinners shall be converted unto thee.

14 Deliver me from bloodguiltiness, O God, thou God of my salvation: and my tongue shall sing aloud of thy righteousness.

15 O Lord, open thou my lips; and my mouth shall shew forth thy praise.

16 For thou desirest not sacrifice; else would I give it: thou delightest not in burnt offering.

17 The sacrifices of God are a

broken spirit: a broken and a contrite heart, O God, thou wilt not despise.

18 Do good in thy good pleasure unto Zion: build thou the walls of Jerusalem.

19 Then shalt thou be pleased with the sacrifices of righteousness, with burnt offering and whole burnt offering: then shall they offer bullocks upon thine altar.

SELECTION 7.

ISAIAH 42: 1-12.

1 Behold my servant, whom I uphold; mine elect, in whom my soul delighteth; I have put my Spirit upon him: he shall bring forth judgment to the Gentiles.

2 He shall not cry, nor lift up, nor cause his voice to be heard in the street.

3 A bruised reed shall he not break, and the smoking flax shall he not quench: he shall bring forth judgment unto truth.

4 He shall not fail nor be discouraged, till he have set judgment in the earth: and the isles shall wait for his law.

5 Thus saith God the Lord, he that created the heavens, and stretched them out; he that spread forth the earth, and that which cometh out of it; he that giveth breath unto the people upon it, and spirit to them that walk therein:

6 I the Lord have called thee in righteousness, and will hold thine hand, and will keep thee, and give thee for a covenant of the people, for a light of the Gentiles;

7 To open the blind eyes, to bring out the prisoners from the prison, and them that sit in darkness out of the prison house.

8 I am the Lord; that is my name: and my glory will I not give to another, neither my praise to graven images.

9 Behold, the former things are come to pass, and new things do I declare: before they spring forth I tell you of them.

10 Sing unto the Lord a new song, and his praise from the end of the earth, ye that go down to the sea, and all that is therein; the isles, and the inhabitants thereof.

11 Let the wilderness and the cities thereof lift up their voice, the villages that Kedar doth inhabit: let the inhabitants of the rock sing, let them shout from the top of the mountains.

12 Let them give glory unto the Lord, and declare his praise in the islands.

ISAIAH 53.

1 Who hath believed our report? and to whom is the arm of the Lord revealed?

2 For he shall grow up before him as a tender plant, and as a root out of a dry ground: he hath no form nor comeliness; and when we shall see him, there is no beauty that we should desire him.

3 He is despised and rejected of men; a man of sorrows, and acquainted with grief: and we hid as it were our faces from him; he was despised, and we esteemed him not.

4 Surely he hath borne our griefs, and carried our sorrows: yet we did esteem him stricken, smitten of God, and afflicted.

5 But he was wounded for our transgressions, he was bruised for our

iniquities: the chastisement of our peace was upon him; and with his stripes we are healed.

6 All we like sheep have gone astray; we have turned every one to his own way; and the Lord hath laid on him the iniquity of us all.

7 He was oppressed, and he was afflicted, yet he opened not his mouth: he is brought as a lamb to the slaughter, and as a sheep before her shearers is dumb, so he openeth not his mouth.

8 He was taken from prison and from judgment: and who shall declare his generation? for he was cut off out of the land of the living: for the transgression of my people was he stricken.

9 And he made his grave with the wicked, and with the rich in his death; because he had done no violence, neither was any deceit in his mouth.

10 Yet is pleased the Lord to bruise him; he hath put him to grief: when thou shalt make his soul an offering for sin, he shall see his seed, he shall prolong his days, and the pleasure of the Lord shall prosper in his hand.

11 He shall see the travail of his soul, and shall be satisfied: by his knowledge shall my righteous servant justify many; for he shall bear their iniquities.

12 Therefore will I divide him a portion with the great, and he shall divide the spoil with the strong; because he hath poured out his soul unto death: and he was numbered with the transgressors; and he bare the sin of many, and made intercession for the transgressors.

SELECTION 8.

ISAIAH 55.

1 Ho, every one that thirsteth, come ye to the waters, and he that hath no money; come ye, buy, and eat; yea, come, buy wine and milk without money and without price.

2 Wherefore do ye spend money for that which is not bread? and your labor for that which satisfieth not? Hearken diligently unto me, and eat ye that which is good, and let your soul delight itself in fatness.

3 Incline your ear, and come unto me: hear, and your soul shall live; and I will make an everlasting covenant with you, even the sure mercies of David.

4 Behold, I have given him for a witness to the people, a leader and commander to the people.

5 Behold, thou shalt call a nation that thou knowest not, and nations that knew not thee shall run unto thee, because of the Lord thy God, and for the Holy One of Israel; for he hath glorified thee.

6 Seek ye the Lord while he may be found, call ye upon him while he is near:

7 Let the wicked forsake his way, and the unrighteous man his thoughts: and let him return unto the Lord, and he will have mercy upon him; and to our God, for he will abundantly pardon.

8 For my thoughts are not your thoughts, neither are your ways my ways, saith the Lord.

9 For as the heavens are higher than the earth, so are my ways higher than your ways, and my thoughts than your thoughts.

10 For as the rain cometh down, and the snow from heaven, and returneth not thither, but watereth the earth, and maketh it bring forth and

bud, that it may give seed to the sower, and bread to the eater:

11 So shall my word be that goeth forth out of my mouth: it shall not return unto me void, but it shall accomplish that which I please, and it shall prosper in the thing whereto I sent it.

12 For ye shall go out with joy, and be led forth with peace: the mountains and the hills shall break forth before you into singing, and all the trees of the field shall clap their hands.

13 Instead of the thorn shall come up the fir tree, and instead of the brier shall come up the myrtle tree: and it shall be to the Lord for a name, for an everlasting sign that shall not be cut off.

SELECTION 9.

Isaiah 60: 1-20.

1 Arise, shine; for thy light is come, and the glory of the Lord is risen upon thee.

2 For, behold, the darkness shall cover the earth, and gross darkness the people: but the Lord shall arise upon thee, and his glory shall be seen upon thee.

3 And the Gentiles shall come to thy light, and kings to the brightness of thy rising.

4 Lift up thine eyes round about, and see: all they gather themselves together, they come to thee: thy sons shall come from far, and thy daughters shall be nursed at thy side.

5 Then thou shalt see, and flow together, and thine heart shall fear, and be enlarged; because the abundance of the sea shall be converted unto thee, **the forces of the Gentiles shall come unto thee.**

6 The multitude of camels shall cover thee, the dromedaries of Midian and Ephah; all they from Sheba shall come: they shall bring gold and incense; and they shall shew forth the praises of the Lord.

7 All the flocks of Kedar shall be gathered together unto thee, the rams of Nebaioth shall minister unto thee: they shall come up with acceptance on mine altar, and I will glorify the house of my glory.

8 Who are these that fly as a cloud, and as the doves to their windows?

9 Surely the isles shall wait for me, and the ships of Tarshish first, to bring thy sons from far, their silver and their gold with them, unto the name of the Lord thy God, and to the Holy One of Israel, because he hath glorified thee.

10 And the sons of strangers shall build up thy walls, and their kings shall minister unto thee: for in my wrath I smote thee, but in my favor have I had mercy on thee.

11 Therefore thy gates shall be open continually; they shall not be shut day nor night; that men may bring unto thee the forces of the Gentiles, and that their kings may be brought.

12 For the nation and kingdom that will not serve thee shall perish; yea, those nations shall be utterly wasted.

13 The glory of Lebanon shall come unto thee, the fir tree, the pine tree, and the box together, to beautify the place of my sanctuary; and I will make the place of my feet glorious.

14 The sons also of them that afflicted thee shall come bending unto thee: and all they that despised thee shall bow themselves down at the soles of thy feet; and they shall **call thee,**

The city of the Lord, The Zion of the Holy One of Israel.

15 Whereas thou hast been forsaken and hated, so that no man went through thee, I will make thee an eternal excellence, a joy of many generations.

16 Thou shalt also suck the milk of the Gentiles, and shalt suck the breast of kings: and thou shalt know that I the Lord am thy Saviour and thy Redeemer, the Mighty One of Jacob.

17 For brass I will bring gold, and for iron I will bring silver, and for wood brass, and for stones iron: I will also make thy officers peace, and thine exactors righteousness.

18 Violence shall no more be heard in thy land, wasting nor destruction within thy borders; but thou shalt call thy walls Salvation, and thy gates Praise.

19 The sun shall be no more thy light by day; neither for brightness shall the moon give light unto thee; but the Lord shall be unto thee an everlasting light, and thy God thy glory.

20 Thy sun shall no more go down; neither shall thy moon withdraw itself: for the Lord shall be thine everlasting light, and the days of thy mourning shall be ended.

ISAIAH 61: 1-7.

1 The Spirit of the Lord God is upon me; because the Lord hath anointed me to preach good tidings unto the meek; he hath sent me to bind up the brokenhearted, to proclaim liberty to the captives, and the opening of the prison to them that are bound;

2 To proclaim the acceptable year of the Lord, and the day of vengeance of our God; to comfort all that mourn;

3 To appoint unto them that mourn in Zion, to give unto them beauty for ashes, the oil of joy for mourning, the garment of praise for the spirit of heaviness; that they might be called trees of righteousness, the planting of the Lord, that he might be glorified.

4 And they shall build the old wastes, they shall raise up the former desolations, and they shall repair the waste cities, the desolations of many generations.

5 And strangers shall stand and feed your flocks, and the sons of the alien shall be your ploughmen and your vinedressers.

6 But ye shall be named the Priests of the Lord: men shall call you the Ministers of our God: ye shall eat the riches of the Gentiles, and in their glory shall ye boast yourselves.

7 For your shame ye shall have double; and for confusion they shall rejoice in their portion: therefore in their land they shall possess the double: everlasting joy shall be unto them.

SELECTION 10.

MATTHEW 5: 1-16.

1 And seeing the multitudes, he went up into a mountain: and when he was set, his disciples came unto him:

2 And he opened his mouth, and taught them, saying,

3 Blessed are the poor in spirit: for their's is the kingdom of heaven.

4 Blessed are they that mourn: for they shall be comforted.

5 Blessed are the meek: for they shall inherit the earth.

6 Blessed are they which do hunger and thirst after righteousness: for they shall be filled.

7 Blessed are the merciful: for they shall obtain mercy.

8 Blessed are the pure in heart: for they shall see God.

9 Blessed are the peacemakers: for they shall be called the children of God.

10 Blessed are they which are persecuted for righteousness' sake: for theirs is the kingdom of heaven.

11 Blessed are ye, when men shall revile you, and persecute you, and shall say all manner of evil against you falsely, for my sake.

12 Rejoice, and be exceeding glad: for great is your reward in heaven: for so persecuted they the prophets which were before you.

13 Ye are the salt of the earth: but if the salt have lost his savour, wherewith shall it be salted? it is thenceforth good for nothing, but to be cast out, and to be trodden under foot of men.

14 Ye are the light of the world. A city that is set on a hill cannot be hid.

15 Neither do men light a candle, and put it under a bushel, but on a candlestick; and it giveth light unto all that are in the house.

16 Let your light so shine before men, that they may see your good works, and glorify your Father which is in heaven.

MATTHEW 7: 1-20.

1 Judge not, that ye be not judged.

2 For with what judgment ye judge, ye shall be judged: and with what measure ye mete, it shall be measured to you again.

3 And why beholdest thou the mote that is in thy brother's eye, but considerest not the beam that is in thine own eye?

4 Or how wilt thou say to thy brother, Let me pull out the mote out of thine eye; and, behold, a beam is in thine own eye?

5 Thou hypocrite, first cast out the beam out of thine own eye; and then shalt thou see clearly to cast out the mote out of thy brother's eye.

6 Give not that which is holy unto the dogs, neither cast ye your pearls before swine, lest they trample them under their feet, and turn again and rend you.

7 Ask, and it shall be given you; seek, and ye shall find; knock, and it shall be opened unto you:

8 For every one that asketh receiveth; and he that seeketh findeth; and to him that knocketh it shall be opened.

9 Or what man is there of you, whom if his son ask bread, will he give him a stone?

10 Or if he ask a fish, will he give him a serpent?

11 If ye, then, being evil, know how to give good gifts unto your children, how much more shall your Father which is in heaven give good things to them that ask him?

12 Therefore all things whatsoever ye would that men should do to you, do ye even so to them: for this is the law and the prophets.

13 Enter ye in at the strait gate: for wide is the gate, and broad is the way, that leadeth to destruction, and many there be which go in thereat:

14 Because strait is the gate, and narrow is the way, which leadeth unto life, and few there be that find it.

15 Beware of false prophets, which

come to you in sheep's clothing, but inwardly they are ravening wolves.

16 Ye shall know them by their fruits. Do men gather grapes of thorns, or figs of thistles?

17 Even so every good tree bringeth forth good fruit; but a corrupt tree bringeth forth evil fruit.

18 A good tree cannot bring forth evil fruit, neither can a corrupt tree bring forth good fruit.

19 Every tree that bringeth not forth good fruit is hewn down, and cast into the fire.

20 Wherefore by their fruits ye shall know them.

SELECTION 11.

JOHN 15: 1-17.

1 I am the true vine, and my Father is the husbandman.

2 Every branch in me that beareth not fruit he taketh away: and every branch that beareth fruit, he purgeth it, that it may bring forth more fruit.

3 Now ye are clean through the word which I have spoken unto you.

4 Abide in me, and I in you. As the branch cannot bear fruit of itself, except it abide in the vine; no more can ye, except ye abide in me.

5 I am the vine, ye are the branches. He that abideth in me, and I in him, the same bringeth forth much fruit; for without me ye can do nothing.

6 If a man abide not in me, he is cast forth as a branch, and is withered; and men gather them, and cast them into the fire, and they are burned.

7 If ye abide in me, and my words abide in you, ye shall ask what ye will, and it shall be done unto you.

8 Herein is my Father glorified,

that ye bear much fruit; so shall ye be my disciples.

9 As the Father hath loved me, so have I loved you: continue ye in my love.

10 If ye keep my commandments, ye shall abide in my love; even as I have kept my Father's commandments, and abide in His love.

11 These things have I spoken unto you, that my joy might remain in you, and that your joy might be full.

12 This is my commandment, That ye love one another, as I have loved you.

13 Greater love hath no man than this, that a man lay down his life for his friends.

14 Ye are my friends, if ye do whatsoever I command you.

15 Henceforth I call you not servants; for the servant knoweth not what his lord doeth: but I have called you friends; for all things that I have heard of my Father I have made known unto you.

16 Ye have not chosen me, but I have chosen you, and ordained you, that ye should go and bring forth fruit, and that your fruit should remain; that whatsoever ye shall ask of the Father in my name, he may give it you.

17 These things I command you, that ye love one another.

SELECTION 12.

REVELATION 21: 1-14, 21-27.

1 And I saw a new heaven and a new earth: for the first heaven and the first earth were passed away; and there was no more sea.

2 And I John saw the holy city, new Jerusalem, coming down from

God out of heaven, prepared as a bride adorned for her husband.

3 And I heard a great voice out of heaven saying, Behold, the tabernacle of God is with men, and he will dwell with them, and they shall be his people, and God himself shall be with them, and be their God.

4 And God shall wipe away all tears from their eyes; and there shall be no more death, neither sorrow, nor crying, neither shall there be any more pain: for the former things are passed away.

5 And he that sat upon the throne said, Behold, I make all things new. And he said unto me, Write: for these words are true and faithful.

6 And he said unto me, It is done. I am Alpha and Omega, the beginning and the end. I will give unto him that is athirst of the fountain of the water of life freely.

7 He that overcometh shall inherit all things; and I will be his God, and he shall be my son.

8 But the fearful, and unbelieving, and the abominable, and murderers, and whoremongers, and sorcerers, and idolaters, and all liars, shall have their part in the lake which burneth with fire and brimstone: which is the second death.

9 And there came unto me one of the seven angels which had the seven vials full of the seven last plagues, and talked with me, saying, Come hither, I will shew thee the bride, the Lamb's wife.

10 And he carried me away in the spirit to a great and high mountain, and shewed me that great city, the holy Jerusalem, descending out of heaven from God,

11 Having the glory of God: and her light was like unto a stone most precious, even like a jasper stone, clear as crystal;

12 And had a wall great and high, and had twelve gates, and at the gates twelve angels, and names written thereon, which are the names of the twelve tribes of the children of Israel:

13 On the east three gates; on the north three gates; on the south three gates; and on the west three gates.

14 And the wall of the city had twelve foundations, and in them the names of the twelve apostles of the Lamb.

* * * * *

21 And the twelve gates were twelve pearls; every several gate was of one pearl: and the street of the city was pure gold, as it were transparent glass.

22 And I saw no temple therein: for the Lord God Almighty and the Lamb are the temple of it.

23 And the city had no need of the sun, neither of the moon, to shine in it: for the glory of God did lighten it, and the Lamb is the light thereof

24 And the nations of them which are saved shall walk in the light of it: and the kings of the earth do bring their glory and honor into it.

25 And the gates of it shall not be shut at all by day: for there shall be no night there.

26 And they shall bring the glory and honor of the nations into it.

27 And there shall in no wise enter into it any thing that defileth, neither whatsoever worketh abomination, or maketh a lie: but they which are written in the Lamb's book of life.

REVELATION 22.

1 And he shewed me a pure river of water of life, clear as crystal, proceeding out of the throne of God and of the Lamb.

2 In the midst of the street of it, and on either side of the river, was there the tree of life, which bare twelve manner of fruits, and yielded her fruit every month: and the leaves of the tree were for the healing of the nations.

3 And there shall be no more curse: but the throne of God and of the Lamb shall be in it; and his servants shall serve him:

4 And they shall see his face; and his name shall be in their foreheads.

5 And there shall be no night there; and they need no candle, neither light of the sun; for the Lord God giveth them light: and they shall reign for ever and ever.

6 And he said unto me, These sayings are faithful and true: and the Lord God of the holy prophets sent his angel to shew unto his servants the things which must shortly be done.

7 Behold, I come quickly: blessed is he that keepeth the sayings of the prophecy of this book.

8 And I John saw these things, and heard them. And when I had heard and seen, I fell down to worship before the feet of the angel which shewed me these things.

9 Then saith he unto me, See thou do it not: for I am thy fellow servant, and of thy brethren the prophets, and of them which keep the sayings of this book: worship God.

10 And he saith unto me, Seal not the sayings of the prophecy of this book: for the time is at hand.

11 He that is unjust, let him be un-just still: and he which is filthy, let him be filthy still: and he that is righteous, let him be righteous still: and he that is holy, let him be holy still.

12 And, behold, I come quickly; and my reward is with me, to give every man according as his work shall be.

13 I am Alpha and Omega, the beginning and the end, the first and the last.

14 Blessed are they that do his commandments, that they may have right to the tree of life, and may enter in through the gates into the city.

15 For without are dogs, and sorcerers, and whoremongers, and murderers, and idolaters, and whosoever loveth and maketh a lie.

16 I Jesus have sent mine angel to testify unto you these things in the churches. I am the root and the offspring of David, and the bright and morning star.

17 And the Spirit and the bride say, Come. And let him that heareth say, Come. And let him that is athirst come. And whosoever will, let him take the water of life freely.

18 For I testify unto every man that heareth the words of the prophecy of this book, If any man shall add unto these things, God shall add unto him the plagues that are written in this book:

19 And if any man shall take away from the words of the book of this prophecy, God shall take away his part out of the book of life, and out of the holy city, and from the things which are written in this book.

20 He which testifieth these things saith, Surely I come quickly: Amen. Even so, come, Lord Jesus.

21 The grace of our Lord Jesus Christ be with you all. Amen.

INDEX.

Titles in SMALL CAPITALS; First lines in Roman; Choruses in *Italics*.

221

INDEX TO RESPONSIVE SCRIPTURE READINGS.